OLD TESTAMENT COMMENTARY SURVEY

JOHN GOLDINGAY

WITH ADDITIONS AND EDITING BY
MARK BRANSON AND ROBERT HUBBARD

FIRST AMERICAN EDITION COPYRIGHT 1977,
SECOND EDITION COPYRIGHT 1981 - THEOLOGICAL
STUDENTS FELLOWSHIP, A DIVISION OF INTER-VARSITY
CHRISTIAN FELLOWSHIP, 233 LANGDON, MADISON, WI 53703

PREFACE TO THE 1975 EDITION

The primary aim of these notes is to survey and comment on the resources available in English for understanding the significance of the OT today. That is, they have in mind the preacher rather than the student working for a degree, though most works likely to be referred to by the student receive some mention. References to periodical articles, however, are confined to some of general interest for the message of the books.

In drawing up this survey, I have made use of an earlier set of Personal Suggestions about a Minister's Library: OT Commentaries, by TSF. I have also referred to the annual Society for OT Study Booklist; to the series of commentary surveys in Theology 60-67 (1957-64); to A.F. Walls' A Guide to Christian Reading (2nd edition, 1961); to D.F. Payne's article on OT Commentaries in English since 1950' in TSF Bulletin 56 (1970); and to various surveys of works on the OT by C.E. Armerding in Christianity Today. I have not tried to cover systematically the classic commentaries of the precritical era (except ones that have been reprinted in recent times); Dr. J.I. Packer's Biblical Exposition: A Bibliographical Guide (2nd edition, 1962) lists many of these, as does C.H. Spurgeon's A Guide to Commentaries (BoT.), while Spurgeon's Commenting and Commentaries (1876, BoT.) provides a detailed and entertaining survey with comments. I am also grateful to members of the Tyndale Fellowship for comments on these comments about commentaries.

Where I have included reference to works which I have not personally used, I have marked these with an asterisk. But whether the opinions are my own or someone else's, they are subjective. Try to avoid making them the sole basis for spending your money on books that you may find useless. The commentaries referred to are of many different critical and theological standpoints. Commentaries are commended to the reader for their positive value in assisting OT interpretation, although basic assumptions made by authors are not necessarily adhered to by the present writer. The reader should, as always, be discerning - try to use the books in a library to see what you make of them yourself for instance. Remember the story about the

professor who told his students that 10% of what he said was wrong; the
trouble was, he didn't know which 10%. Please let me know (at St. John's
College, Bramcote, Nottingham) if you think I am wrong about matters of fact
or matters of opinion, or if I have omitted important works.

This survey was completed in summer 1974 and updated early in 1975.
Listing book prices is like trying to board a moving bus, but we have done
our best. Dates generally refer to when the book was first published in
English (or significantly revised), but remaining details (publisher, etc.)
refer to the most recent edition.

In the actual commentary section, titles are omitted where they are
straightforward (e.g.Genesis, The Book of Genesis, Genesis: A Commentary)
and authors' names are underlined. Thus U. Cassuto refers to U. Cassuto
Commentary on the Book of Genesis.

Nottingham   John Goldingay

PREFACE TO THE AMERICAN EDITION OF 1981

Professor Goldingay's 1975 edition has been supplemented by Robert Hubbard.
At my request, TSF of England has granted us permission to revise this publication
so that (1) American publishers would be included; (2) a few additions could be
made, and (3) the rapidly fluctuating prices could be omitted. (They seldom remained
accurate long enough for us to publish them before they went up!) Any section with
a (+) will be supplemented in the Appendix beginning on page 48. All section
headings and numbers are matched for easy reference.

Robert Hubbard of Denver Seminary has served as an Associate Editor with TSF
for five years. Sally Asperger and Terri Olson have spent hours researching publishers
and typing the manuscript. Inter-Varsity Press has provided art work and printing.
My work of coordinating these efforts and of editing the various products has been
most worthwhile personally and I hope, pastorally. Students and ministers can more
easily make use of these excellent resources. You can help us by sending any

comments you may have to me. Although I did little of the actual writing of this survey, I must take responsibility for the final choices made in editing. (Probabl. not wise for one more studied in theology!) Be sure to follow _Themelios_ and _TSF Bulletin_ so you can keep abreast of more recent works.

Madison, Wisconsin

Mark Lau Branson
TSF General Secretary

ABBREVIATIONS

AB	Anchor Bible (Doubleday)
BoT	Banner of Truth
CB	Century Bible (Frowde)
CBSC	Cambridge Bible for Schools and Colleges (CUP)
CBC	Cambridge Bible Commentary on the NEB (CUP)
CUP	Cambridge University Press
EB	Expositor's Bible
EPC	Epworth Preacher's Commentaries
h/b	hardback
IB	Interpreter's Bible (Abingdon)
ICC	International Critical Commentary (Clark/Scribners)
IVP	Inter-Varsity Press
LC	Layman's Bible Commentaries (John Knox)
NBC	New Bible Commentary (Eerdmans)
NCB	New Century Bible (Oliphants/Attic)
NICOT	New International Commentary on the OT (Eerdmans)
o/p	out of print
OUP	Oxford University Press
OTL	Old Testament Library (Westminster)
p/b	paperback
RBC	Religious Book Club (SCM/Allenson)
SBT	Studies in Biblical Theology (SCM)
s/h	second hand
TB	Torch Bible Commentaries (Allenson)
TEF	Theological Education Fund Study Guides (SPCK/Allenson)
TOTC	Tyndale OT Commentaries (IVP)
WC	Westminster Commentaries (Allenson)

v

CONTENTS

1. THE FUNCTIONS OF COMMENTARIES

The concerns of commentaries are varied. They may include

a) The textual: establishing what the Bible in its original language actually said; helping one to choose between variant readings and to assess suggested emendations.

b) The literary: investigating the historical origin and background of the text, its sources, the literary genres or types it exemplifies, the process of its growth before it reached written form, and the changes made to this oral form by those who put it into writing.

c) The linguistic: translating the text and/or elucidating the meaning of particular words or sentences. This shades into

d) The exegetical, in the narrow sense: ascertaining the text's meaning, and what it refers to, against its historical, geographical, cultic, and social/cultural background,

e) The kerygmatic: I use this term to denote the endeavour to understand what particular message the text was seeking to bring to the original readers, what its purpose was. This needs to be distinguished from

f) The theological: seeing the particular theological issues, words, and concepts referred to or raised by the text against their wider OT and Biblical background.

> (A book's message and its theology are strictly speaking
> part of the concern of the exegete: but in practice
> they are often not treated as such.)

g) The expository: extrapolating from the message the text brought; the message God would bring us now.

Understandably, few commentaries even attempt this whole range of topics. But ones that concentrate primarily on literary and historical matters, for instance (as many have done) will be of less value for the preacher. On the other hand, there is no road to the kerygmatic and the theological except via the linguistic, the historical, and so on; and in particular

expository commentaries that are not founded on topics a) to
f) are like buildings erected on sand.

2. GENERAL RESOURCES

2. GENERAL RESOURCES

General works that deal systematically with one of the above areas supplement
commentaries and make it less important for the latter to cover all the
topics.

a) The text:[+] The British and Foreign Bible Society Hebrew Bible, edited by
N.H. Snaith (1958) is a convenient and adequate edition of the standard
Ben Asher text. Perhaps even more convenient is Bagster's Hebrew and English
OT - the original with translation alongside! The standard critical text
will now be Biblia Hebraica Stuttgartensia edited by K. Elliger and W.
Rudolph (Württembergische Bibelanstalt, Stuttgart; about 14 parts, to be
combined in one volume, 1968 on), succeeding Kittel's Biblia Hebraica
(3rd edition, 1937 same press).

D.R. Ap-Thomas's A Primer of OT Text Criticism (1947, Fortress Press)
is that, while E. Wurthwein The Text of the OT (1957) is a more advanced
work - but both are dated. Fortress Press has released Textual Criticism
of the OT (1974) by R. Klein as one of their 'Guides to Biblical Scholarship'.
Volumes such as these help to explain the translations' marginal notes and
the differences between translations, as well as illuminating the principles
upon which commentators may also be working. For ascertaining the NEB's
emendations (as the Library Edition indicates them) L.H. Brockington's
The Hebrew Text of the NEB (1973 CUP) may be worth referring to though not
buying.

b) Literary Questions:[+] The various OT Introductions deal systematically with
these. The new one by J. Soggin (OTL 1976) now looks the most useful, as
it combines a lucid coverage of the technical questions with a consideration of the background and message of each book. E. Mellor's The Making of

the OT (CBS 1972) opens up the general questions in a simpler way. Longer but still digestible introductions to these are provided by the Fortress Press 'Guides to Biblical Scholarship', Literary Criticism of the OT (N.C. Habel 1971), Form Criticism of the OT (G.M. Tucker, 1972), and Tradition History and the OT (W.E. Rast, 1972). The latter two areas are also dealt with by K. Koch in The Growth of the Biblical Tradition (1969, Westminster). General treatment of these questions and of others concerning the origin, history and interpretation of the Bible is provided in the three volumes of the Cambridge History of the Bible (1963-70 CUP).

Apart from R.K. Harrison's encyclopedic Introduction to the OT (1969 IVP) there is little on this difficult area written from a more conservative viewpoint. But note G.E. Ladd's The NT and Criticism (1970 Eerdmans) for an exposition of why these questions are important to someone who has this perspective and of how they may be approached. This may they be applied to the OT. History, Criticism, and Faith edited by Colin Brown (1977, IVP) supplements Ladd's book by dealing with crucial issues in both OT and NT criticism.

c) Language and translation:+ Brown, Driver and Briggs; Hebrew and English Lexicon of the OT (Houghton, M &Co, 1907) remains standard, pending the completion of the long promised new Oxford lexicon. There is a shorter but more up-to-date one by W.L. Holladay,* A Concise Hebrew and Aramaic Lexicon (1971, Eerdmans) and very brief ones by G. Fohrer (1973 SCM) and A. Souter (De Gruyter). But these latter two tell you little you could not infer from the English translations!

J. Strong's* Exhaustive Concordance (Abingdon) and R. Young's Analytical Concordance (Eerdmans), are the best English concordances. Get one with a solid binding, but not India paper (which makes it difficult to use). Young usefully subdivides entries under English words (e.g. 'sacrifice'), according to which word was used in the original (zebah, minhah, etc) and also lists at the back the various English translations of

each Hebrew word (e.g. for minhah 'gift', 'oblation', 'offering', etc) so
that you can look up other passages that use the same word even though the
English translation is different (It is, however, based on the A.V. -
there is no OT concordance based on a more modern translation). Bagster's
Englishman's Hebrew and Chaldee Concordance does this for you by listing
words in the main body of the book by the Hebrew words (e.g. all the oc-
curences of minhah come together) - the actual entries then being in English
(hence the title). The concordances of *G. Lisowsky (1958 Württembergische
Bibelanstalt) and *S. Mandelkern (ed. M.H. Goshen-Gottstein, Shalom) prints
the entries themselves in Hebrew. The former is easier to use.

It will be particularly important for the non-Hebraist to have as
adequate as possible translations of the OT. Despite the popularity of the
RSV, the RV, or the related American Standard Version is still valuable for
study purposes, because of its literalness and its refusal to emend the
text. Not that one would use it in the pulpit or refuse to accept emendation;
but at least with the RV the non-Hebraist is as close as possible to our
point of departure, the traditional Hebrew text. RSV, NEB, JB, and the
other modern translations are all freer in their emendation and/or their
translation; they thus embody interpretations of the text to a greater
extent and prejudge the work of the commentator/exegete. The complete
TEV is now available and is very helpful. The New International Version
should be completed soon and promises to be worthwhile.

d) Exegesis and background:[+] Bible Dictionaries may be mentioned under this
heading, though they will have a contribution to make in other areas. The
New Bible Dictionary (2nd edition J.D. Douglas et al., 1962 Eerdmans)
provides a useful basic coverage especially as regards archaeological and
historical questions. Much vaster is The Interpreter's Dictionary of the
Bible (ed. G.A. Buttrick et al, 1963 Abingdon), perhaps the modern equivalent
to Hastings' Dictionary of the Bible (1898-1904), which is still worth
picking up s/h. A supplementary volume to the IDB is now available. The
one-volume Hastings (1909) has appeared in a completely new version edited

by F.C. Grant and H.H. Rowley (1963 Clark). General background to the OT
is also provided by two CBC introductory volumes, Understanding the OT
(CUP) and OT Illustrations (CUP 1971). Understanding the OT by B.W. Anderson
(3rd edition, 1975 Prentice-Hall) has been valued by many as an all-
purpose guide to the history, literature and faith of Isreal.

The historical reference of the OT, of central importance in areas
such as Kings, will be elucidated by a book such as J. Bright's A History of
Israel (OTL 1972), though the shorter volumes of F.F. Bruce (Israel and
the Nations 1963 Eerdmans), R.K. Harrison (OT Times 1970 Eerdmans), or
D.F. Hinson (History of Israel 1973 Allenson) usually cover the subject well
enough for the preacher. Such books usually cover relevant archaeological
material (Bright and Harrison especially), but there are many useful hand-
books that concentrate on the archaeological background to the OT. Among
recent ones are E. Yamauchi The Stones and the Scriptures (1972 Lippincot),
J.A. Thompson The Bible and Archaeology (2nd edition 1973 Eerdmans), and
H.T. Frank An Archaeological Companion to the Bible (1972 Abingdon).
D. Winton Thomas's Documents from OT Times (1958 Harper and Row) usefully
collects written material from the ancient near east which illustrates
the background to OT history, religion, literature etc.

The geographical reference of the OT is of central importance
in books such as Joshua. Although the maps in a bible dictionary or a
book such as Bright will generally suffice, an atlas with comprehensive
indexes is a worthwhile investment. H.G. May's *Oxford Bible Atlas
(2nd edition, 1974 OUP) is a good value, as is Blaiklock's Zondervan
Pictorial Bible Atlas (1972) and the Aharoni and Avi-yonah's Macmillan
Bible Atlas (1968). Also helpful is Denis Baly's revised Geography
of the Holy Land (1974 Harper and Row) or G.A. Smith's classic Historical
Geography of the Holy Land (25th edition 1931 Peter Smith, probably available s/h). Aharoni has also published *Land of the Bible (1967 Westminster).

The cultic reference (e.g. Leviticus, Chronicles) will be covered by

books on Israel's religion/worship - e.g. H.H. Rowley Worship in Ancient
Israel (1967 Allenson), H. Ringgren Israelite Religion (1966 Fortress) or
H.J. Kraus Worship in Israel (1966 Blackwell). G. Fohrer History of
Israelite Religion (1973 Abingdon) and Th.C. Vriezen Religion of Ancient
Israel (1967 Westminster) should also be mentioned.

The social/cultural background (e.g. patriarchs, Judges-Samuel,
prophets) will be elucidated especially by R. de Vaux Ancient Israel (1961
McGraw) and J. Pedersen's classic Israel (1926-40 OUP) - both of these cover
the cult as well. E.W. Heaton's Everyday Life in OT Times (1956) has recently
been re-issued at a bargain price (Scribners).

e) The Message of the biblical books: An older book which should be mentioned is
C. Westermann's A Thousand Years and a Day (1966 Fortress), an easily written
survey of the OT books drawing attention to ways in which they speak to the
modern world. G.von Rad's OT Theology (1962-65 Harper and Row) works through
the distinctive messages of the various OT books; the preacher will find
this a mine of insight though von Rad's exposition is tied up with radical
positions on OT criticism. Volume 2, also published separately as The Message
of the Prophets (1968 Harper and Row), is easier to use, yet in some ways
volume 1 is even more valuable for its attempt to see the message of the
pentateuch, the histories and the writings. E. Voegelin's Order and
History I, Israel and Revelation (1956 Louisiana State University) is a
theological history of the OT period in the von Rad tradition, full of insight
on the OT books and deserving to be better known than it is. P.R. Ackroyd's
Exile and Restoration (1968 Westminster) deals with the theological concerns
of the books he connects with the period of the exile and restoration again,
here, there is much insight (including an especially thorough treatment of
the restoration prophets), though it is a difficult book. Zimmerli has
written two non-technical introductions to the OT message - Man and His Hope
in the OT (1971 Allenson) and The Worldliness of the OT (1976 John Knox). A
valuable older evangelical work that belongs under this heading is G. Vos

Biblical Theology (Eerdmans, reprinted 1975); the first three-quarters
is a historical treatment of the OT revelation.

The Archbishop of York, Stuart Blanch, has written two books on the
Bible that are substantially about the message of OT books in today's
world, The World Our Orphanage (Epworth 1972) and For all Mankind (Bible
Reading Fellowship 1976). W.C. Kaiser in The OT in Contemporary Preaching
(Baker 1973) similarly introduces many aspects of the different parts of the
OT, trying to bridge the gap between us and parts that seem difficult. A
literary approach to the Bible, which examines the text itself to see what
its own concerns are, is becoming an important focus of OT study. See,
for instance, U. Simon's Story and Faith in the Biblical Narrative (Allenson
1975); and, for general introductions from this angle by conservative
writers, L. Ryken The Literature of the Bible (Zondervan 1974) or KRR Gros
Louis (ed), Literary Interpretations of Biblical Narratives (Abingdon 1974).

Work showing much scholarly insight into the message of the OT books
has appeared over the past decade or so in journals. More especially the
series on the 'kerygma' of various books in Interpretation in the 1960's -
well worth xeroxing!

f) Theology: + The 'cross-section' theologies help one to see passages in their
significance against the total context of OT thinking. Eichrodt (1961 Westminster) and Vriezen (2nd edition, 1966 Branford) are probably the most helpful.
Note also the OT sections in the Kittel Theological Dictionary of the NT
(9 volumes 1964-74 Eerdmans) but also now the Theological Dictionary of the OT ed.
Botterweck and Ringgren, 4 volumes of 12 now out, Eerdmans).

If you can't aspire to these, you can possess such volumes as Alan
Richardson's Theological Wordbook (1950 Macmillan), von Allmen's Vocabulary
of the Bible (1958 Lutterworth) Edgar Jones' Greatest OT Words (1964 SCM),
and Girdlestone's Synonyms of the OT (2nd edition 1897 Eerdmans - outdated in
places): There is a further wordbook by Jones, *God, Man and Community (1974

John Paul). A cross between wordbook and theology is N.H. Snaith's very valuable
The Distinctive Ideas of the OT (1944 Schocken).

There is a conservative volume by J.B. Payne, Theology of the Older
Testament (Zondervan). H.W. Wolff's Anthropology of the OT (Fortress 1974)
is a most valuable examination of the OT understanding of man. J. Ellul's
The Meaning of the City (Eerdmans 1970) is a wide-ranging study of the
phenomenon of civilization and urbanization in the light of the Bible,
suggestive in its use of Genesis, Psalms, and prophets. J. Rogerson's The
Supernatural in the OT (Lutterworth 1976) helpfully examines the way the OT
speaks of the activity of God in the world, though his conclusions may not at
every point commend themselves to a conservative reader. G.F. Hasel OT Theology:
Basic Issues in the Current Debate (Eerdmans 1975) is a wide ranging thorough
survey.

g) Exposition: The preacher will profit from some treatment of principles of
interpretation. A.M. Stibbs' Expounding God's Word (revised, 1976 IVP)
and Understanding God's Word (1950) retain their value though they
antedate the modern hermeneutical debate. On typology, see D.L. Baker's
thesis Two Testaments, One Bible (1977 IVP) and his article in Scottish
Journal of Theology 29 (1976 137-57). Much older, but still instructive,
are P. Fairbairn's The Interpretation of Prophesy (1856) and The Typology
of Scripture (reprinted by Baker) which help one to avoid excesses in either
of these difficult areas. The modern debate has raised more questions so
far than answers, but it does warn against simplistic approaches as well as
suggesting pointers for a right Christian use of the OT. John Bright's
Authority of the OT has been reissued by Baker. Other works on the use of
the OT which might be mentioned are W. Wink The Bible and Human Transfor-
mation (Fortress 1973), a paperback which tries to get beyond biblical
criticism without going back on it; A.T. Hanson Studies in Paul's Technique
and Theology (Eerdmans 1974), a series of very technical studies followed by

a more intelligible discussion of the Christian use of the OT; J.M.
Robinson and J.R. Cobb The New Hermeneutic (Harper 1964), a useful intro-
duction to this movement; A.A. van Ruler The Christian Church and the OT
(Eerdmans 1971), an independent and suggestive contribution; B.S. Childs
Biblical Theology in Crisis (Westminster 1970), is an excellent volume which
includes a survey and statement of the principles put into practice in his
commentary on Exodus; E. Achtemeier The OT and the Proclamation of the
Gospel (Westminster 1973) and F.R. McCurley Proclaiming the Promise:
Christian Preaching from the OT (Fortress 1974), more surveys with practical
suggestions as to how to go about preaching the OT. Also, see J. Barr
Old and New in Interpretation (Harper and Row 1966) and The Bible in the
Modern World (1973 SCM); C. Westermann (ed.) Essays in OT Interpretation/
Hermeneutics (1963 John Knox); B.W. Anderson (ed.) The OT and Christian
Faith (Harper and Row 1963); J.D. Smart The Interpretation of Scripture
(Westminster 1961) and The Strange Silence of the Bible in the Church
(Westminster 1970); A. Richardson Religion in Contemporary Debate (1966 SCM)
ch 4-5.

3. ONE VOLUME COMMENTARIES AND SERIES[+]

a) The New Bible Commentary Revised (ed. D. Guthrie et al. 3rd edition
Eerdmans 1970) provides a useful basic exegesis from an evangelical perspective, though it is of course brief.

Peake's Commentary, the 'new Peake' published in 1962 (ed. M. Black and
H.H. Rowley, Nelson reprinting 1975) does a similar job from a more mixed
viewpoint and on a considerably bigger scale. It is more academic in the
good and the bad senses. I have particularly valued the treatments of
Exodus, Psalms, Isaiah, Daniel.

b) *The Interpreter's One Volume Commentary (ed. C.M. Laymon 1971 Abingdon) is less substantial than Peake.

The Jerome Bible Commentary (ed. R.E. Brown et al 1968 Prentice-Hall) is a substancial RC volume (though its origin does not very often affect the treatment offered).

The Interpreter's Bible (ed. G.A. Buttrick, Abingdon 6 OT Volumes 1952-56) provides good introduction, moderate length exegesis and also an exposition - but the latter are almost uniformly disappointing; and with these and the printing of AV and RSV at the top of each page and awful lot of paper is wasted. Nevertheless the general increase in the price of commentaries means that these volumes do not look as expensive as they did some years ago and the whole set may be worth buying. On some books (Joshua, Job, Isaiah 40-66, some of the minor prophets) the IB remains as good as anything else available.

The Broadman Bible Commentary (ed. C.J. Allen, 7 OT volumes 1969-73 Broadman) is a new fairly conservative Baptist exegetical commentary, much briefer however than IB and without scope for a verse-by-verse treatment. It is in fact not much longer than the less imposing, and perhaps unfortunately titled

Layman's Bible Commentaries (14 OT Volumes 1959-66 p/b SCM, now mostly o/p, h/b John Knox). These offer a chapter-by-chapter exegesis which always keeps one eye on the theological/kerygmatic/expository. Especially valuable for the less commentated books. The paperbacks remain a bargain if you can pick them up.

The Scripture Union Bible Study Books (8 OT volumes 1967-71) are a similar but shorter evangelical series, with proportionately less exegesis and more devotional application. Also published with additional introductory material as The Daily Commentary (2 h/b volumes 1974). SU also publish a devotional series on Bible Characters & Doctrines (12 volumes).

c) Distinguishable from the above multi-volume unified treatments of the OT are the various commentary series, whose individual volumes will be mentioned under the books concerned. A word about the general ethos of the series may, however, be said here.

The Anchor Bible (Doubleday) is a self-consciously ecumenical, non-confessional series which normally offers a thorough introduction, a new translation and linguistic and exegetical notes - usually brief in the case of the longer books. Inclined to be dry.

The Cambridge Bible Commentary on the NEB (CUP) is a rather brief and inevitably simplistic, exegetical series, with some concern however for religious and theological issues. Aimed at sixth forms and colleges of education. Rather expensive for what they are.

The Epworth Preachers Commentaries were a series of brief exegetical and expository volumes, now o/p.

The New Century Bible (Oliphants, formerly Nelson) is almost the British equivalent to the AB. A moderately detailed exegesis from a mainstream critical position. Not generally showing a theological, kerygmatic, or still less expository concern. Again, rather dry.

The Old Testament Library (Westminster) is a solid modern series of rather mixed ethos. Some are fairly narrowly historical/critical; but many (mostly ones translated from Das Alte Testament Deutsch) are most valuable for their theological exegesis and elucidation of the writer's religious message. The series includes some of the most exciting commentary work of this century.

The Torch Bible Commentaries (SCM now mostly only available as p/b some o/p) are a briefer exegetical series, many of which keep one eye on the theological/kerygmatic.

The Tyndale Old Testament Commentaries (IVP) are a similar, though perhaps slightly more detailed, series but by conservative scholars.

The Theological Education Fund Study Guides (SPCK p/b) cover various biblical books; produced with the church overseas in mind, they outline a mainstream exegetical position and by means of questions etc., suggest lines of application to today's world. Illustrated.

Hermeneia (Fortress Press) is a new series of substantial commentaries that
promises translations of some of the famous volumes in the Biblischer
Kommentar Altes Testament (e.g. Zimmerli on Exekiel, Wolff on Hosea, Amos,
and Joel) - a series of massive commentaries that pays as much attention to
the books' message and theology and Christian significance as it does to
literary and linguistic questions - as well as new works (Talmon on Ezra
fairly soon, B.W. Anderson on Genesis, N. Lohfink on Deuteronomy, etc.).

d) Older comprehensive works and series are listed in chronological order:

Luther's Works (Fortress or Concordia) includes translations of his lectures
on Genesis (8 volumes!), Deuteronomy, Selected Psalms (3 volumes),
Ecclesiastes/Song of Solomon/Last Words of David, Isaiah 1-39 and 40-66
and minor prophets (3 vols). I find Luther more of a Christian expositor
than an exegete.

Calvin's Commentaries (Eerdmans) reveal him as an extraordinary combination
of the historical exegete and the expositor. Of course his exegesis and the
application to his own day need updating; but he remains most stimulating.
His commentaries cover Genesis to Joshua, Psalms, and Isaiah to Malachi
in 30 volumes (sometimes available s/h but mostly in print with Eerdmans).

Matthew Poole's Commentary (BoT 1975) is a quite detailed verse-by-verse
exegetical work with a particular concern for elucidating difficulties
and explaining apparent contradictions.

Matthew Henry's Commentary (1706-12 6 OT volumes; Revell, whole Bible in
1 volume) is more concerned with exposition and was in fact intended to
complement Poole; it can still be suggestive.

Keil and Delitzsch produced a most scholarly conservative technical commentary on the Hebrew text in the 1860's (s/h or Eerdmans, 10 volumes).
There is no more modern conservative equivalent and they are still valuable
used alongside more recent textual and linguistic work.

Lange's Commentary (14 OT volumes) is the IB of the 1860's/1870's; thorough textual, exegetical, theological and homiletic treatment of the English text. Difficult to come by but worth referring to if you have access to a set.

Jamieson, Faussett and Brown (Marshall) is the NBC of 1871. Valuable for its mediation of much other nineteenth century conservative work.

The Cambridge Bible for Schools and Colleges which the CBC replaces, spanned the period from 1880 to the First War and thus began before the critical revolution in Britain. They gave a competent linguistic and exegetical treatment of most of the OT and remain useful, though of course need checking. The earlier volumes were later revised or replaced with ones based on the RV which were, however, not manifestly superior!

*Ellicott's Bible Commentary (5 OT volumes) and *The Pulpit Commentary (14 OT volumes Zondervan or Eerdmans) were both conservative reactions to the advances of 'Wellhausenism'. The former is exegetical, the latter also expository.

F.B. Meyer's expositions of biblical characters (Marshall) also have their origin in this period, though they show no knowledge of critical work. They tend to be exegetically shaky and excessively typological and are dated devotionally as well as exegetically, The same goes for Alexander Whyte's Bible Characters: OT (Zondervan). The Expositor's Bible also belongs to the 1880's/1890's. It was a valiant attempt at an expostion which was based firmly on the best (incipiently critical) exegesis of the day. Inevitably both the exposition and its exegetical base have dated, but some volumes remain useful and the whole endeavor provides a model for us. Easily obtained s/h.

Alexander Maclaren's Expositions (c. 1904-8 Baker) are more eclectic in their choice of text and less well grounded in exegesis, though Maclaren's presuppositions were similar to those of the EB (11 OT volumes).

The International Critical Commentary (1895 on, Clark / Scribners, but easily obtained s/h) belongs to the period when the critical battle was over. There is no more recent and as thorough treatment of text, language etc. though it is often very dated.

The Century Bible is a brief series from the turn of the century briefer even than CBSB and generally not as useful.

The Westminster Commentaries, begun about 1899, are exegetical and are really the NCB of the period. They describe themselves as less elementary than CBSB, less critical than ICC, and less didactic than EB - which is true enough. Dull and dated on the whole.

The Devotional Commentary included some OT volumes; again they had rather little exegetical base and even the application is dated.

e) Commentaries in foreign languages are not dealt with in these notes; it may just be worth noting that there are some very valuable volumes in the German series Das Alte Testament Deutsch and the Biblischer Kommentar, though many have been or are being translated, and in the French series Etudes Bibliques, Sources Bibliques and Commentaires de l'AT.

4. COMMENTARIES BOOK BY BOOK - THE PENTATEUCH +

For the past hundred years there has been debate over the authorship and origin of the pentateuch. Most of the books mentioned below assume that the pentateuch includes material from various sources (J E D P etc), which was only put together in the postexilic period. Many of the books also use form criticism and tradition criticism to trace the history of the material before it even reached these sources and their conclusions on these matters obviously affect their interpretation of the text (e.g. books by von Rad, Noth, Ellis, Childs), If you question their critical views you may also question their exegesis! Some of the books maintain an essentially conservative view, dating the material nearer the time of Moses (e.g. works by Kidner, Cassuto, Cole, Thompson, Leupold, Kline) as of course do the older works (e.g. Luther, Calvin, Meyer, Griffith Thomas).

Orientation to these questions is provided by the standard 'OT Introductions' or the works mentioned in paragraph 2 (b), which generally accept the JEDP approach. For alternative views see R.K. Harrison's Introduction to the Old Testament (Eerdmans) or K.A. Kitchen Ancient Orient and OT (1966 IVP) and Pentateuchal Criticism and Interpretation (TSF). A more sympathetic treatment by a conservative is R.J. Thompson Moses and the Law (Leiden Brill). W. Brueggemann and H.W. Wolff The Vitality of Old Testament Traditions (John Knox 1975) is a set of valuable articles on the message of J, E, D, and P: like Ellis's work, valuable even if you don't believe in J, E, D, and P!

GENESIS +

U. Cassuto (1961-64 Magnes Press, Hebrew University, Jerusalem) is the most detailed modern exegetical commentary though covering only chapters 1-13; it is original not to say idiosyncratic and discursive. J. Skinner (1910 Allenson) can thus still be useful. Less thorough but up-to-date is E.A. Speiser (AB 1964), which has an excellent introduction and linguistic notes and full treatment of relevant archaeological discoveries which provide important background both to Genesis 1-11 and to the patriarchs. S.R. Driver (Allenson 1904) is still of some exegetical value and worth picking up. There is also some exegetical help in the conservative volume of H.C. Leupold (1953 Baker) though it has a dated air and the suggested homiletic applications are not very imaginative.

There are many theological/kerygmatic treatments of Genesis beginning with Luther and Calvin who wear their years well here. Of the modern ones, the most famous, the most stimulating, the most original and the most full of insight if G. von Rad (OTL 1961 3rd edition 1972). Von Rad's theological exposition is worked out in conjunction with his work on tradition history; this means, as with his Theology, that the former may need reconsidering if his critical views are questioned. N.M. Sarna (Understanding Genesis 1966 Schocken) offers essentially a popularizing of von Rad's theological approach and Speiser's use of archaeology - very good value for money. F.D. Kidner's more conservative approach (TOTC 1967) well complements Sarna and von Rad. Kidner is deceptively pithy - every sentence is worth weighing; and he always sets Genesis in its widest biblical context. So does Alan Richardson's theological commentary (i.e. it has less exegetical detail than Kidner, which is more of a general purpose volume) on Genesis 1-11 (TB 1953); but Richardson infers (mistakenly, in my opinion) from the undoubted presence of symbolic ways of speaking in these chapters, that they mean to be taken as only parables of universal human experience and not as also relating, in figurative terms indeed, once-for-all events at far off stages of man's history. This vitiates his theological exposition. A.S. Herbert completes the TB treatment of Genesis (1962); his volume is useful but rather brief. R. Davidson (CBC 1973) is a similar approach to Genesis 1-11 as that of Richardson and is on a similar scale though it both gains and loses through being written by a professional OT scholar rather than a professional theologian. H. Thielicke How the World Began (1964 Fortress) expounds Genesis 1-11 to modern man in a powerful way. J. Hargreaves (1969 TEF, Allenson) boils down and synthesises the currently common exegetical approach and provides many hints for applying it. *B. Vawter A Path through Genesis (1957 Sheed & Ward) is a quite substantial Roman Catholic treatment of the book; H. Renckens Israel's Concept of the Beginning (Herder & Herder, NY 1964) and C. Hauret Beginnings (1964 Christian Classics) both provide discursive and thought-provoking theological exegesis of Genesis 1-3 from a Roman Catholic standpoint. Carlos Mesters Eden: Golden Age or Goad to Action? (Orbis 1974) is a stimulating re-reading of Genesis 1-3 with a liberation theology atmosphere. D. Bonhoeffer's exposition of these first three chapters in Creation and Fall (Macmillan 1959) like Richardson's commentary is written by a theologian rather than an OT scholar; it tends to read rather more into the text than is really there. E.J. Young's

exegetical and devotional study of Genesis 3 (Presby & Reformed 1966)
is also discursive but rather predictable. Of other devotional/homiletic
treatments *M. Dods (EB 1892) and W.H. Griffith Thomas (DC 1909 Eerdmans)
are among the better of their respective series and are worth picking up
cheaply though needing to be checked by more recent exegetical work.
G. Lawson's The History of Joseph (1807-12 BoT) is a verse-by-verse exposition of Genesis 37-50 suggesting lessons for Christian living (e.g.
50:11 indicates that we should remember when mourning that our behaviour will
be observed by others). J. Hercus' treatment of Joseph in Pages from God's
Casebook (1962 IVP) runs less risk of eisegesis and speaks more to modern
man. Francis Schaeffer's Genesis in Space and Time (1972 Regal) also has
a modern feel; he valuably stresses the historical actuality of the Genesis
events, as his title implies, though he is very literalist and also in
danger of eisegesis through assuming that Genesis is answering exactly
the questions that we want to ask. D.F. Payne's Tyndale Monograph Genesis
One Reconsidered (Tyndale Press 1964) provides a valuable corrective to this.
Claus Westermann has written two works on these opening chapters The
Genesis Accounts of Creation (1964 Fortress Press) and a more substantial
volume on Creation (1974 Fortress Press). The former is more exegetical,
the latter more concerned with the significance of the creation story for
modern man - though elucidating this by means of a more penetrating
grasp of Genesis' meaning in its own right. Finally P. Ellis has written
a stimulating interpretation - Genesis: The Yahwist (1968 Fides Publishers).
In the von Rad tradition, this is an illuminating work even if you do not
believe in J! G. Coats' From Canaan to Egypt (CBQ Monograph No. 4)
concerning the Joseph story examines its theology and literary structure.

EXODUS - DEUTERONOMY

Calvin's Harmony of the Four Last Books of the Pentateuch (Eerdmans)

arranges the treatment of the various laws under the ten commandments as
Calvin sees the former as itemizing the latter - an interesting exercise
in itself, though the rearrangement makes the commentary complicated to use
(there is, however, an index at the end) and it obscures the arguments of
individual chapters and sections. But Calvin's theological exegesis of
these books remains of great value, especially in the absence of more modern
attempts at this in commentaries. There are, however, several chapter-by-
chapter expositions of the pentateuch: e.g. *W.H. Griffith Thomas Through
the Pentateuch (Eerdmans), OT Allis God Spake by Moses (1951 Presby &
Reformed - describing itself as an exposition but doing what I would call
more exegesis), F.B. Meyer The Five Books of Moses (Christian Literature)
(Meyer is better, in my opinion, when working through the text than in his
character studies). They are not very recent, but can still be suggestive.

Several studies of Moses may be mentioned: M. Buber (Harper & Row
1946) includes much theological exegesis of Exodus/Numbers; so does G.
von Rad (1960) though more briefly, but adding chapters on the commandments
and the law. Andre Neher (A.S. Barnes 1959) like Buber, provides a Jewish
treatment, in his case more of an overt exposition of the significance of
Moses for the Jewish people; a sensitive and thought-provoking work.

On the significance of the ten commandments, there are works of
several types to mention. J.J. Stamm and M.E. Andrew include considerable
exegetical material in their survey of The Ten Commandments in Recent
Research (SBT 1967). This will provide a useful check on the wide ranging
exposition of Thoman Watson The Ten Commandments (1692, Depot 1959) and
other expository works, ancient and modern. In Hard Sayings (1972 Eerdmans)
F.D. Kidner offers a succinct summary of the challenge of the OT's moral
teaching, grouping the material largely around the commandments, while
A. Phillips on a larger scale examines the commandments and the teaching of
much of the laws in a more exegetical study, Ancient Israel's Criminal Law
(1970 Schocken). D. McCarthy's Old Testament Covenant (1972 Knox) surveys

current discussion including the Decalogue.

EXODUS +

J.P. Hyatt (NBC 1971) is the most thorough treatment of critical,
historical, geographical and cultic questions, in the rather dull tradition
of A.H. McNeile (London: Methuen 1908) and S.R. Driver (Putnam 1911).
R.E. Clements (CUP 1972) is similar but briefer. Not as brief, because they
do not have to incorporate the actual text, and with more concern for the
theological/kerygmatic are G. Henton Davies (SCM 1967) and R.A. Cole (IVP
1973), which are complementary. U. Cassuto's large scale commentary
(1967 Magnes Press, Hebrew University, Jerusalem) often manifests a
considerable literary feel and sensitivity to the book's message and is
helpful for exegesis; like his commentary on Genesis, it is original/
idiosyncratic. In The God of Exodus (1966 Bruce, Milwaukee) J. Plastaras
in fact offers a historical exegesis with some theological treatment of
most narrative parts of Exodus and some of Numbers and Deuteronomy, as does
D.M. Beegle (though also with more of a literary concern) in Moses (1973
Eerdmans). F.B. Meyer (DC 1911-13) is suggestive and better based exeget-
ically than his character studies tend to be, but H. Law The Gospel in
Exodus (BoT) is allegorical: the burning bush speaks of the suffering of
Christ and also of his overcoming them. J. Hercus includes a study of
Pharaoh in Pages from God's Casebook (1962 IVP). At another extreme M.
Noth (Westminster 1962) is almost exclusively concerned with literary
questions and offers little help; but its successor in the OTL series by
B.S. Childs is a different kind of volume altogether (1974). Despite its
blurb, it does consider textual, literary, philological and historical
questions, but it then goes on to consider passages' significance within
the context of the OT, how they are used in the NT, how they have been
interpreted and applied since and what theological reflection we might

make on the basis of them now. A most stimulating work. E. Nicholson's
Exodus and Sinai in History and Tradition (1973 Knox) takes up the higher
critical question of the relationship of the Exodus and Sinai.

LEVITICUS[+], NUMBERS

Get the LC volume by J.L. Mays (1963) before the English edition goes
o/p! The standard critical commentary is N.H. Snaith (NCB 1967), which
concentrates on such matters as the nature and background of the religious
institutions described but does not go on to their theological significance.
Snaith's views may be ascertained from the briefer treatment of these books
which he provided for the revised Peake. J.R. Porter CBC (1976) is a
welcome addition to its series since this is an under-commentated book.
A sympathetic approach concerned to understand Leviticus in its own right,
though in my opinion narrow in its approach to the meaning of many of the
laws. M. Noth's two volumes (OTL 1965-68) are similar to Snaith though they
also consider literary questions more thoroughly and end up even drier.
On the other hand, on Leviticus A. Bonar (1846 Carter & Bros) is fanciful
in the extent to which he typologizes and the answer to the question of the
theological significance of such books cannot lie here; S.H. Kellogg
(Armstrong 1891) is more sober, and the CBSC volume by A.T. Chapman and
A.W. Streane (Putnam 1914) is worth picking up for exegesis. Note also
books on OT worship, sacrifice etc and Bible Dictionaries. On Numbers there
is a thorough ICC volume by G.B. Gray (1903 Allenson) and briefer ones by
A.H. McNeile (CBSC 1911) and L. Elliott-Binns (London: Metnuen 1927) –
though I have the impression that these older volumes on Leviticus and
Numbers (except Kellogg) appear rather infrequently s/h. On the theology
and interpretation of Numbers there were some useful articles in Interpretation 13.1 (1959). IB's exegesis of Numbers is useful. In the CBC,
Sturdy is due on Numbers.

DEUTERONOMY +

A first look at J.A. Thompson's TOTC volume (1974 IVP) suggests that
it is a careful, open-minded piece of exegesis which keeps half an eye
on the book's significance in the light of the NT. P.C. Craigie New
International Commentary (Eerdmans 1976) has now appeared: a large volume
by a well-informed conservative writer. For an older yet thorough linguistic and exegetical commentary see the ICC volume by S.R. Driver (Scribner's
Sons 1895) though this needs supplementing on the linguistic side and in the
light of new insights on the covenant and laws gained through ancient near
eastern treaty parallels which especially affect Deuteronomy. A thorough-
going attempt to interpret Deuteronomy in the light of these was made by
*M.G. Kline in The Treaty of the Great King (1963 Eerdmans) but R.E. Clements
also draws attention to them in his useful 'theological interpretation of
the book of Deuteronomy', God's Chosen People (Allenson 1968). M.
Weinfeld Deuteronomy and the Deuteronomic School (OUP 1972) raises many
aspects of the theology of Deuteronomy in connection with an investigation
of its background and origins. H. Cunluffe-Jones' commentary (TB 1951)
is a useful volume majoring more on the book's message, its theology and
its abiding significance than on detailed exegesis, though it is inclined to
sit in judgement on what it sees as the book's limitaions and it antedates
the discovery of the treaty parallels, as does the otherwise useful exegesis
by G.E. Wright in IB. G. von Rad's commentary (OTL 1966) has a high
reputation as a kerygmatic/theological exposition, though I have not
myself found it as illuminating as his work on Genesis; but note also his
series of essays opening up theological themes Studies in Deuteronomy
(Westminster 1953). There have been various articles in Interpretation
on the message/theology of Deuteronomy 6.3 (1952), 19.4 (1965), 22.4 (1968),
23.4 (1969), and the whole issue 15.1 (1961). The older commentaries of
G.A. Smith (Putnam 1918) can still be useful, as can H. Wheeler Robinson's
brief exegesis (NY: Frowde 1907); there is a new short commentary by

*A.C J. Phillips (CUP 1973); and a volume of *Luther's lectures in the
Concordia series.

5. THE 'HISTORIES'

JOSHUA[+]

    J. Soggin (1972) is one of the less useful OTL volumes as far as the
preacher is concerned; it majors on literary questions and has a rather
negative estimate of the historical value of the book. The same is true
of J. Gray (Joshua, Judges and Ruth Attic 1967), though treating quite
thoroughly matters of language, geography and social customs. The CBC
volume by J.M.Miller and G.M. Tucker (1974 CUP) is of a similar ethos but
briefer. The CB volume on Deuteronomy by H.W. Robinson (Frowde) also
includes Joshua, but there is more detailed exegesis in the (original)
CBSC commentary by G.F. Maclear (1878 CUP). For help in discerning the
book's theological/kerygmatic/expository significance - apart from a
valuable 4 page section in Soggin's introduction - there is an article on
the Deuteronomic theology in Joshua by G. Wenham in JBL 90.2 (1971); though,
on the theological significance generally of the salvation history story
also see the appropriate sections of von Rad's Theology I. and of Voegelin,
For something on a larger scale, we have to turn back to Calvin. A.W.
Pink's Gleanings in Joshua (Moody) jump so soon into the NT and spend so
much of their time there that they don't really seem to be a treatment of
the OT book. F.A. Schaeffer Joshua and the flow of Biblical History (IVP
1975) is a series of straightforward Bible readings, independent of
scholarly study of the book; just rescued from the bathos of many devotional
treatments of books such as Joshua by the breadth of Schaeffer's theological
vision.

JUDGES [+]

On Gray see under 'Joshua'; there are also thorough older technical
works by G.F. Moore (ICC 1895) and C.F. Burney (c.1919 Ktav, with Kings)·
but A.E. Cundall (TOTC 1968) gives a quite adequate coverage of history,
exegesis etc., Cundall takes his work on the message of Judges a stage
further in an article on "Judges - An Apology for the Monarchy" in
Expository Times 81.6 (1969-70); there is further light on Judges' place
in salvation history in von Rad and Voegelin and a more systematic treatment
in M. Buber's Kingship of God (Harper & Row 1967). J.D. Martin CBC (1975)
is briefer than Cundall and similar in approach, though less conservative.
R.G. Boling (Doubleday 1975) is an original commentary (which means one
finds oneself asking 'Did the Biblical author really mean that/did the book
really come into being that way?) with a concern for the message of the
stories and of the book as a whole, and with thought-provoking titles for
the sections. There is an article on the significance of chapters 13-14
in Interpretation 27.1 (1973). J. Hercus in God is God (1971 Hodder) offers
a more existential, racy, un-put-downable retelling of the Judges stories
which both makes them live and keeps underlining the involvement of God
in these very secular-sounding, modern events and people.

RUTH [+]

L. Morris adds an exegesis of Ruth to Cundall's treatment of Judges
(Judges and Ruth 1968 IVP). G.A.F. Knight offers a more theological/
kerygmatic exegesis of Ruth and Jonah (SCM 1950) - insightful and thought
provoking. R.M. Hal's The Theology of the Book of Ruth (1969 Fortress Press)
expounds that subject exhaustively, perhaps finding more there than there
is! On J. Gray see under Joshua. W.J. Fuerst has written a very useful
short commentary on the Five Scrolls Ruth, Esther, Ecclesiastes, Song of
Songs, Lamentations (CUP 1975). A sympathetic and helpful introduction to

some difficult books. E.F. Campbell has written a detailed commentary
(Doubleday 1975).

SAMUEL[+]

   With the historical books generally, unlike the prophets, there is
not very much problem about the meaning of the text, though historical and
geographical references may need elucidating. The preacher will, however,
value help with how these books are to be preached. Thus, among the
collection of worthwhile modern commentaries on Samuel, he will probably
appreciate most H.W. Hertzberg's treatment which gives prominence to the
kerygmatic themes (OTL 1964). W. McKane (TB 1964) also pays attention
to the message of the books and his exegesis supplements Hertzberg. P.R.
Ackroyd (1 Samuel CBC 1971, 2 Samuel to follow), likewise seeks to elucidate
the purpose and message of the text; and R.N. Whybray's The Succession
Narrative (Allenson 1968), although - mistakenly, in my judgement -
describing 2 Samuel 9-20, 1 King 1-2 as a historical novel, offers much
insight on the themes of these chapters. J. Hercus provides further
retelling of the story of David (1967 IVP) and of Saul in Pages From
God's Casebook (IVP 1962), which as usual give more realistic pictures of
the man despite whom God works, than the more hagiographic treatments.

   J. Mauchline (Attic Press 1971) is a more traditional exegetical
commentary, concentrating on historical points etc. A.F. Kirkpatrick
(Scholarly 1880) is a similar volume from a century ago. H.P. Smith (ICC
1904) and S.R. Driver (1889) are more technical older volumes. R.A.
Carlson's David the Chosen King (1964 Almqvist and Wiksell, Stockholm) is
'a traditio-historical approach to 2 Samuel' also of value for its textual
comment; close study of it would also, however, I suspect be rewarding for
an understanding of the message of 2 Samuel. The same is true of T.
Campbell's The Ark Narrative (1975 Scholars Press); it offers many

structural insights and theological observations about the Ark in Samuel.

KINGS [+]

J. Gray (OTL 2nd edition 1970) is indispensible, in the corrected
and revised edition, for its treatment of text, language, history, background etc., but it does not venture beyond that and is hardly worth the
preacher's money. Nor are the older technical works of J.F. Montgomery
and H.S. Gehman (one of the more recent ICC volumes 1951, Scribners Sons)
or C.F. Burney (1903 see under 'Judges'). J. Robinson (1 Kings CUP 1972
2 Kings to follow) is brief and of little more help. The CB volume by
J. Skinner (Frowde c. 1893 - with Isaiah) is worth picking up.

On the message of Kings von Rad has a useful chapter on the Kings
theology of history in his Studies in Deuteronomy (SBT 1953); note also the
relevant sections of his Theology and of Voegelin and an article on the
kerygma of these history works in Interpretation 22.4 (1968). H.L. Ellison
The Prophets of Israel (1969 Eerdmans) offers a history of the northern
kingdom (which is the meaning of 'Israel' in the title) especially in
relation to the prophetic movement there. There is a useful expository
treatment of the lives of Elijah and Elisha by R.S. Wallace (Eerdmans 1957)
and others (more dated and exegetically shaky - but still sometimes
illuminating) by F.W. Krummacher, (London), and on Elijah by A.W. Pink
(Moody 1956). But the one 'must' on Kings is Jacques Ellul's The Politics
of God and the Politics of Man (1972 Eerdmans).

CHRONICLES, EZRA, NEHEMIAH [+]

P.R. Ackroyd (Allenson 1973) and J.M. Myers (Doubleday 1965, 3
volumes) have produced splended volumes looking at the Chronicler's message
in its own right, rather than as merely a source for information to sup-

plement that in Kings. Ackroyd is especially good on redaction criticism, and his volume will obviously have the edge financially. Myers has good introductions. R.J. Coggins has completed the two CBC volumes. M.D. Goulder Midrash and Lection in Matthew (!) (Allenson 1974) includes valuable material on Chronicles - Ezra - Nehemiah. An article on the theology and message of the Chronicler appeared in Biblical Theology Bulletin 5.2 (1975) by Goldingay. L.H. Brockington (Ezra, Nehemiah and Esther 1969 Attic Press) is more exclusively concerned with historical and background questions and is not very helpful for the preacher. Similarly there are the two older volumes in the ICC, E.L. Curtis and A.A. Madsen (Chronicles 1910 Allenson) and L.W. Batten (Ezra and Nehemiah 1913 Allenson). On Nehemiah, Alan Redpath wrote a devotional study which corresponds to the intention of the book it expounds better than many character studies of this type Victorious Christian Service (1959 Revell).

ESTHER +

C.A. Moore (Doubleday 1971) has written a thorough modern commentary, replacing L.B. Paton (Allenson 1908); but the preacher will probably be satisfied if he can pick up G.A.F. Knight's fairly sympathetic theological commentary (Esther, Song of Songs, Lamentations, Macmillan 1955). On L.H. Brockington see under 'Chronicles, Ezra, Nehemiah'. On Fuerst, see under 'Ruth'.

In Four Strange Books (1967 Schocken) E. Bickerman, who is a classical scholar also interested in Judaism, looks at four books - Daniel, Ecclesiastes and Jonah as well as Esther - presumed to come from the Greek age, and provides some original insights on their background and meaning, thought and aims. The chapter on Esther also has interesting material on the history of the book's interpretation (including the Greek Esther) but also an idiosyncratic theory as to the book's origin.

6. THE POETICAL BOOKS [+]

On the wisdom books G. von Rad's last book <u>Wisdom in Israel</u> (Abingdon 1972)
developing the seminal thoughts in his <u>Theology I</u>, is the standard theological guide. W. Brueggemann flies a large number of kites in <u>In Man
We Trust</u> (1972 J. Knox) - as the very title implies, it is an attempt to
expound the wisdom tradition's gospel as this appears especially in Proverbs
and as it is embodied in Saul, David, and Solomon. R.B.Y. Scott's <u>The
Way of Wisdom</u> (1971 Macmillam) is a less exciting, more straightforward
introduction. There have been articles on the theological significance
of wisdom by Zimmerli in <u>Scottish Journal of Theology</u> 17 (1964), by D.A.
Hubbard in <u>Tyndale Bulletin</u> (1966) and several in <u>Interpretation</u> 23.3 (1969)
and 24.1 (1970).

JOB [+]

Job offers a double challenge. The first lies in the technical area of
texts and language which raises many problems in this book. What do
individual verses actually say? The second is the need to grasp the thought
of the book, to see the wood for the trees in its arguments. Perhaps a
third challenge should be distinguished, that of tracing the book's literary
history; some approaches to the question of the book's literary integrity
will affect one's understanding of its argument.

The classic commentary is <u>E. Dhorme's</u> massive work (London: Nelson
1967). It has a long introduction and full notes on text and exegesis
(referring to the Hebrew a fair amount), which are marked by a sobriety
which makes them seem less dated than one might expect of a volume published
in 1926 in an area that has been the subject of such vast research since.
There is also still much of abiding value in the textual and linguistic
work of <u>S.R. Driver and G.B. Gray</u> (ICC 1921) and in <u>C.J. Ball's</u> commentary
(1922). All, however, need updating. <u>F.I. Anderson</u> (TOTC 1976) is excellent

because of the author's linguistic talents and passion for clear theology. It's not only the best but, but also a model for others. Another recent solid commentary is M.J. Pope (3rd edition Doubleday 1973): it has a good introduction and verse by verse notes, though little room in the confines of the series to justify the positions taken. H.H. Rowley (Attic Press 1970) is disappointing; he provides a valuable compendium of opinions on the problems, but the average reader will find it difficult to know what to do with the information; and he is little help with the thread of the argument. R. Gordis has written a different kind of volume The Book of God and Man (1965 Chicago UP) which meets the latter need both by a series of valuable essays which summarize and examine the different sections of the book and by the chapter by chapter summaries with which Gordis inter- sperses his translation and notes. A useful volume. Finally among the more substantial treatments one ought to mention S. Terrien in the IB which has a good introduction and a commentary full of insight. Terrien's other work *Job, Poet of existence (Bobbs-Merrill 1957) incorporates the substance of the commentary for the ordinary reader.

Among the shorter exegetical works two useful modern ones are by H.L. Ellison From Tragedy to Triumph (1958 Zondervan); and by A. and M. Hanson (Allenson 1963), though I doubt whether their understanding of the book's theme as the story of a man's being brought from self-vindication to justification by faith is fair to Job! N.C. Habel (CBC 1975) is brief but pithy and suggestive in its approach to old problems of interpretation. (the redeemer passages, wisdom poems, Elihu speeches, Yahweh speeches). The older works of A.B. Davidson (CBSC 1884) and A.S. Peake (CB Frowde) 1965) are also still of value. Again two other recent short treatments of Job offer superb, sensitive running theological commentaries on its message, section-by-section: James Wood's Job and the Human Situation (Bles 1966) and E. Jones' The Triumph of Job (SCM 1966). Similar older volumes were written by H.W. Robinson The Cross of Job (1916 reprinted in The Cross

in the OT 1955 Westminster) and T.H. Robinson Job and His Friends (SCM
1954). All the books in this paragraph appear periodically s/h and any
makes a useful introduction to the book. Also worth mentioning under this
heading are the section on Job in Pedersen's Israel I (1926 OUP), and the
exegetical paragraphs in N.H. Snaith's The Book of Job (Allenson 1968) -
the purpose of this study is to expound an approach to the question of the
book's origin, but there is considerable valuable material on its contents.
Finally H.H. Rowley wrote a characteristically thorough and helpful survey
of approaches to the book in an article reprinted in his From Moses to
Qumran (1963 Books for Libraries). *H.H. Kent's Job Our Contemporary
(Eerdmans 1967) is not a commentary but of use for exposition and applicati
of the book as a whole. D.M. Howard's How Come God? (SU) is another popula
overview.

PSALMS +

Older commentaries can be misleading here. Those such as Spurgeon
(Pilgrim Press) and Dickson are full of devotional insight, but this is not
infrequently unrelated to the text - which affects their usefulness as
guides for the preacher who wishes to expound what the psalms actually
say. The older critical commentaries do not take into consideration the
appreciation of the psalms in their various types in the context of Israel'
worship, which has been developed especially through the work of H. Gunkel
(for an introduction to his work see The Psalms 1967 Fortress Press) and
S. Mowinckel (see the systematic statement of his views in The Psalms in
Israel's Worship Abingdon 1962).

C. Barth offers a general orientation in the light of such approaches
in Introduction to the Psalms (1966 Int. Schol Bk Serv). H. Ringgren's
The Faith of the Psalmists (SCM 1963) which majors more on the theological/
religious themes of the psalms. C. Westermann's more independent volume

The Praise of God in the Psalms (J. Knox 1965), which had its origin in the author's study in prison camp, is full of insight on the theology of Israel's prayer and praise, though at times it is not easy to follow. Three more applied volumes deal with selected psalms. J. Hargreaves (Allenson 1973) starts more from the faith of the psalmists, than from Israel's worship, like Westermann; he takes 20 well known psalms and tries to relate that faith to today in the light of modern psalm study. The other two are B.W. Anderson's Out of the Depths (1974 Westminster), which looks at sample psalms of each of the main types categorized by modern psalm study, considers the theological issues raised for us by them and the ways we may use them. A notable attempt at a scholarly but applied approach.

Among actual commentaries, J.H. Eaton (Allenson 1967) is an introductory commentary which again, following the trend of current psalm study, provides for each psalm an introduction setting it in its place in Israel's worship. In fact Eaton perhaps yields rather too much to the liturgical interpretation. It also gives exegetical notes and a paragraph attempting a Christian interpretation of the Psalms. *C.S. Rodd (Allenson 1963-4) provides an apparently similar short modern theological exposition designed to help the preacher. F.D. Kidner (IVP 1973 2 volumes) yields less to the current scholarly presuppositions and provides a more detailed exegesis. A.F. Kirkpatrick (Macmillan 1902) is also still of value for exegesis, though the question of the psalms origin is not approached from the modern critical standpoint. J.A. Alexander (Baker 1975) is a reprint of a conservative exegetical work of 1850, still of value for its explication of the text itself. Baker/Evangelical Press have in print another conservative commentary by H. Leupold (1972). J.H. Eaton has now followed up his Torch Commentary with a book on Kingship and the Psalms (Allenson 1976) which develops his conviction that many of the psalms were for the king to use. There is considerable theological treatment of the themes of the psalms.

Of the bigger commentaries, older volumes such as <u>C.A. and E.G. Briggs</u> (Allenson 1907 2 volumes) are rather out of date in their attitude to textual questions as well as to questions of origin and meaning (but they are useful for information on Hebrew grammar!) <u>A. Weiser's</u> theological/ kerygmatic commentary (OTL 1962) is full of insight and suggestive for the preacher, though heavily committed to a particular view of the psalms' liturgical background (everything is an aspect of the covenant renewal ceremony). <u>M. Dahood</u> (Doubleday 3 volumes 1966-70) is equally heavily committed to reading the psalms in the light of Ugaritic; it is impossible for the non-specialist to use with discernment. <u>A.A. Anderson</u> (Attic Press 1972 2 volumes) - the best in the NCB series - provides a more balanced detailed exegetical commentary, not over-committed to any particular approach though coming down more on the liturgical side but not opening up questions of exposition. C.S. Lewis' <u>Reflections on the Psalms</u> (1958 Harbrace J.) are in a category of their own, coming from right outside the conventional lines of approach. For that very reason they can be suggestive and stimulating.

PROVERBS

There are some superb treatments of very different kinds. The standard technical commentary now is <u>W. McKane</u> (OTL 1970), very thorough on textual, exegetical, linguistic and formcritical matters and not ignoring the theological; but it is a demanding volume in which the theological treasure is only found by digging deep. Nothing could be more different, except in the matter of size, than <u>C. Bridges</u> (Sovereign Grace Book Club 1959) - nineteenth century homiletic treatment at its best. But <u>F.D. Kidner</u> (IVP 1964) is the commentary most likely to commend itself to the average preacher for its subject studies (the fool, the sluggard, etc.) as well as its useful exegesis. <u>D.R. Jones'</u> similar popular modern treatment

(Proverbs, Ecclesiastes, SCM 1961) is less pithy but often complementary. R.B.Y. Scott (Proverbs, Ecclesiastes, Doubleday 1965) deals with the two books in a less applied way, and his notes are little longer, though he has very useful introductions to the two books and to wisdom literature in general. R.N. Whybray (CUP 1972), the most recent smaller commentary, is not very directly helpful to the preacher. Nor is C.H. Toy (Allenson 1899), though it still has valuable textual and linguistic material. On W. Brueggemann's In Man We Trust, see under 'The Wisdom Books' above. There have been articles on the message/theology of Proverbs in Interpretation 20:1 (1966) and 26:2 (1972).

ECCLESIASTES

On D.R. Jones and R.B.Y. Scott see above under 'Proverbs'. There is no very substantial textual/linguistic commentary in English more recent than G.A. Barton (Allenson 1908), though R. Gordis Koheleth (3rd edition 1968 Schocken) comes closest to this. It has a valuable set of introductory essays and an exegetical commentary (which refers to the Hebrew a fair amount) - a 'best buy'; though E.H. Plumptre's CUP volume (1881) is also worth picking up.

The above all tend to stress the pessimistic tone of the book - 'life is bad, all we can do is submit ourselves to God'. An alternative interpretation in positive terms is made by H. Leupold (Baker) in a competent exegetical commentary which maintains that Ecclesiastes was written as 'counsel for God's people in evil days and times of depression', to encourage them to turn to their God. On Fuerst see under Ruth. A first look at D. Kidner A Time to Mourn, and a Time to Dance (IVP 1976) suggests it manifests Mr. Kidner's consistent pithiness, lightness of touch, and independence in bringing home the hopelessness of life if what the author says is all there is to say.

SONG OF SONGS[+]

R. Gordis (Ktav; Jewish Theological Seminary of America 1954) -
now reissued and combined with Lamentations (Ktav, 1974), again provides a
useful textual/linguistic commentary for a book with many detailed
problems of interpretation. The earlier edition introduced the major question:
of what 'relationship' is the book speaking? To this, introductory notes,
translation, and exegetical notes on the Hebrew text are added as solid contribu-
tions.

A traditional allegorical interpretation - presenting the relationship as between God and man - is the view expounded in detail in
commentaries such as G. Burrowes (1853 BoT), Watchman Nee (1966 Christian
Lit), and Hudson Taylor Union and Communion (Bethany Fellowship c. 1910).
But most modern interpreters take the more obvious view that the poems
describe the love of a man and a woman. G.A.F. Knight Esther, Song of
Songs, Lamentations (Macmillan 1955) provides a convenient brief treatment
along these lines. Glickman's A Song for Lovers (IVP 1976) is a recent
translation, paraphrase with popular comments. There is an essay reviewing
the various approaches to this general problem of interpretation in H.H.
Rowley's The Servant of the Lord and other essays (1952, 2nd edition
Allenson). A. Harper's CBSC volume (1902 Macmillan) is worth picking up
for its exegesis. On Fuerst, see under 'Ruth'.

7. THE PROPHETS [+]

The past hundred years have seen developments in the criticism of
the prophetic books which are parallel to those in relation to the
pentateuch that have been noted above. The older commentaries emphasized
the predictive side of the prophetic books, which is also the interest of
modern writers such as Hal Lindsay and F.A. Tatford. Most modern works
mentioned below, however, assume that the prophets' message was first of

all meant to speak to the concerns of their own day.

The conviction that prophets primarily address their own day led
to the further belief that parts of the books that do not speak to the
prophet's own period must have been added to his collected works. Most
notably Is. 40-66 and indeed much of Is. 1-39 is widely assumed to have been
written in the exile or after. Among books mentioned below, ones that
reflect more conservative views include those by Harrison, Taylor, Ellison,
Young, Leupold, Kissane, and Erlandsson.

The standard modern book on the religious phenomenon of prophecy in
Israel is J. Lindblom's Prophecy in Ancient Israel (1962 Fortress Press)
but this does not very directly serve the needs of the preacher. More
concerned with the theological significance of prophecy are W. Zimmerli
The Law and the Prophets (1965 Gannon) and R.E. Clements Prophecy and
Covenant (Allenson 1965). A.B. Davidson's OT Prophecy (Int. Theological
Library 1903) was an equivalent turn of the century volume which is still
useful for its discussion of the interpretation of predictive prophecy,
of false prophecy, and of messianic prophecy from an early reverently
critical viewpoint.

All these books deal with the subject topically. Ones that introduce
the prophets one-by-one may be more helpful. Of these the modern classic
is von Rad's The Message of the Prophets (Harper & Row 1968) - actually
only another edition of his Theology II (H&R) - which is full of insight
and most suggestive. H.L. Ellison's Men Spake from God (1952 Eerdmans)
is also an independent, though much less imposing work, a useful introduction. On his Prophets of Israel (Zondervan), see above under 'Kings';
it covers Amos, Hosea and Jonah. Like this latter book of Ellison's,
but covering all the prophets to the exile, *N.K. Gottwald's All the
Kingdoms of the Earth (H&R 1964) is especially helpful in relating the
prophets to contemporary history. Stephen Winward's A Guide to the Prophets
(1968 J. Knox) is a more systematically potted guide to the contents of

the books - the kind of work which one suspects can become a substitute for thinking through their message oneself, though that is not the author's fault! A similar older volume is A.F. Kirkpatrick's The Doctrine of the Prophets (1892 Macmillan) - worth picking up cheaply; also W. Robertson Smith's The Prophets of Israel (Appleton 1882) for the eighth century prophets. The persons of Isaiah, Jeremiah and Ezekiel are examined by J. Hercus in More Pages from God's Casebook (IVP 1965).

A book which crosses these two categories of treatment, dealing with the subject partly book by book, partly topically, is A. Heschel's The Prophets (1962 Harper & Row 2 volumes). Heschel's attempt to grasp the essence of what it means to be a prophet has received rave reviews though I confess I have not been able to get into it.

ISAIAH +

There are a number of useful commentaries. In their short compass the TB three are all useful. J. Mauchline (Isaiah 1-39 1962) is a very thorough treatment for its size; it offers considerable exegetical help - as well as showing an openness towards the possibility of an Isaianic connection of much of the material. D.R. Jones (Isaiah 56-66 and Joel 1964) offers a thorough exegesis of the last chapters and points out the Christian significance of them. C.R. North (Isaiah 40-55 1952) is the most dispensable of this trilogy, because this section of the book especially demands more thorough coverage and has received it in other volumes not least by North himself (see below).

The OTL volumes are also notable, both for their exegesis and for their attempt to go on to suggest the abiding significance of the book. Admittedly O. Kaiser (Isaiah 1-12 1972 and Isaiah 13-39 1974) attributes very little even of 'first Isaiah' to Isaiah himself, and the concern with tracing literary history threatens to become overbearing in the second volume, where also he offers less theological help; but the first is a warm and suggestive commentary. So is C. Westermann (Isaiah 40-66 1969 OTL); its particular characteristic is its creative use of form criticism as an aid in exegesis and in giving a feel of the impact of the prophet's message on the hearers.

Several commentaries on the whole book have been written since the war by scholars who believe in the literary unity of Isaiah. The most substantial is *E.J. Young (1965-72 Eerdmans 3 volumes), originally part of the New International Commentary OT series, now distributed separately. It has been described as of considerable linguistic and exegetical value, though making no use of tools such as form criticism. A.S. Herbert (CBC chapters 1-39 1973 and 40-66 1975) is very brief in both volumes yet helpful in exegesis. Also of linguistic and exegetical value are the works of *H.C. Leupold (1968 Baker) and the nineteenth century classic of J.A. Alexander (1846-7 Zondervan), as well as the not anti-critical but just independent work of the Roman Catholic scholar E.J. Kissane (Browne & Nolan 1941-3), and the older brief treatments of J. Skinner (Frowde 1896-8) and, to a lesser extent, O.C. Whitehouse (1905 Frowde). Older still are the expositions of Luther (2 volumes) and Calvin (4); Calvin's masterly treatments of the prophets (though he did not live to complete Ezekiel) are invaluable both for their content and, even where they are wrong exegetically or now dated, as models for the expositor. G.A. Smith wrote an expository commentary on the whole book (Doubleday 1890-96), which has had a very high reputation - beware of inflated s/h prices!

On Isaiah 1-39 there is an expository by *J.Y. Muckle (Epworth 1960) which has been said to be unfortunately influenced by views about the non-Christian nature of the book and about the nature of prophecy. J.M. Ward's Amos and Isaiah (1969 Abingdon) is not a commentary but a discussion of major exegetical and theological issues of the material conventionally attributed to Isaiah of Jerusalem, especially in chapters 1-12. On Isaiah

1-27 <u>G.B. Gray's</u> technical linguistic and exegetical volume (Allenson 1912)
has by no means yet been replaced, though on chapters 13-23, and especially
13-14, S. Erlandsson's <u>The Burden of Babylon</u> (1970 Gleerup, Lund) provides
a very thorough treatment in the course of reopening the question of the
origin of the oracle against Babylon. Finally on Isaiah 1-39, the coverage
in <u>IB</u> and especially in <u>Peake</u> is of above average usefulness.

Isaiah 40-55 has attracted notable commentators of all inclinations.
At one end is the valuable technical commentary on the Hebrew text by <u>C.R.
North</u> <u>The Second Isaiah</u> (Allenson 1964) - not to be treated as the last
word, but the inevitable point of departure for serious study. Then there
are less technical exegetical volumes by <u>J.L. McKenzie</u> <u>Second Isaiah</u>
(Doubleday 1968) and <u>C.C. Torrey</u> <u>Second Isaiah</u> (1928 Scribners Sons) -
an older volume whose distinctive basic approach has influenced more
recent theological works such as those of <u>Simon</u> and <u>Smart</u>, who also think
the Cyrus references are secondary, but whose exegesis is often very helpful. Both of these cover chapters 34-35 and 40-66. Muilenburg's exegesis
in the <u>IB</u> ought also to be mentioned. Then there is the famous survey
of <u>The Suffering Servant in Deutero-Isaiah</u> by C.R. North (Allenson 1948);
as a survey of current opinion this is now out of date, and it was always
as much of curiosity value as anything else for the oddity of some of the
views it reported, but there is valuable material on the actual exegesis
of the servant passages. H.H. Rowley's survey article covers the subject
more briefly (<u>The Servant of the Lord and other essays</u> 1950 2nd edition
1965 Allenson; the 'other essays' include one on 'The Suffering Servant
and the Davidic Messiah' also relevant to this theme). It too is dated
but here again there are valuable exegetical points. Finally on the Servant
should be mentioned H. Wheeler Robinson's <u>The Cross of the Servant</u> (1926
reprinted in <u>The Cross in the OT</u> 1955 OTL). On Isaiah 40-66 <u>R.N. Whybray</u>
(Attic Press 1975) offers a general purpose volume, majoring on verse-by-
verse elucidation of textual and exegetical question. H. Blocher expounds

The Songs of the Servant (IVP 1975) in the light of their fulfilment in Christ: a model of devotional exposition with a scholarly mind underlying it. P. Holmgren With Wing as Eagles, Biblical (Scholars Press, New York 1973) is 'an interpretation' of Isaiah 40-55 which emphasizes its exposition of Yahweh's relationship to Israel as King, Holy One, Saviour, and Mighty One.

The expository/theological volumes are U.E. Simon's A Theology of Salvation (1953 SPCK), G.A.F. Knight's Deutero-Isaiah 'a theological commentary on Isaiah 40-55' (1965 Abingdon), and J.D. Smart's History and Theology in Second Isaiah (i.e. chapters 35 and 40-66) (1965 Westminster). All are polemical, excited and hopefully exciting volumes, which make traditional exegetes sit uneasy in their chairs. As Knight notes, they need to be read alongside an exegetical commentary; one must not be swept along by the oratory. A more straightforward small expository commentary is that of S.C. Thexton (1965 SCM) which has some suggestive ideas for preaching.

JEREMIAH +

There is no satisfying commentary on Jeremiah. J. Bright (Doubleday 1965) is the fullest modern one, and even that is thin, especially on the theological/kerygmatic side. As usual with the AB, it has a thorough introduction, however. If this volume is ultimately disappointing, this is perhaps because of the limitations of size and aim placed upon it by the nature of the series (rather than Bright's lack of insight!). Like Bright E.A. Leslie (1954 Abingdon) rearranges the material into a presumed more chronological order (which begs the question of the significance of the order that appears in the book); he then offers a not very complicated running commentary on the paragraphs of the book. H. Cunliffe-Jones (Allenson 1960) and R.K. Harrison (IVP 1973) offer similar shorter commentaries, helpful primarily on question of history etc. <u>E.W. Nicholson's</u> two CBC volumes (1973-5) are of value for understanding the significance of the book passage by passage, when allowance is made for their brevity. There is a large conservative commentary by <u>T. Laetsch</u> (Concordia 1952). F. Schaeffer in <u>Death in the City</u> (IVP 1969) offers suggestive application of Jeremiah and Lamentations to modern man. W. Holladay <u>Jeremiah:</u> <u>Spokesman out of Time</u> (United Church Press, Pa 1974) examines aspects of the interpretation of the book and of its application to today. <u>A.S. Peake</u> (Frowde 1911-12) is an older commentary of the same kind.

Belonging to the same period as this last is a whole series of books on the person and message of Jeremiah, of which the most famous is J. Skinner's <u>Prophecy and Religion</u> (CUP 1922): valuable for helping one to get the thrust of significant aspects of Jeremiah, though (like other books of the time and since) attributing disproportionate significance to his 'individualism'. There are similar books by <u>G.A. Smith</u> (Doran 1923), <u>W.F. Lofthouse</u> (SCM 1925) and <u>A.C. Welch</u> (Macmillan 1951) and a more recent one by *<u>S.H. Blank</u> (1961 Hebrew Union College Press, Cincinnati). Rather narrower, but deep, is H.W. Robinson's <u>The Cross of Jeremiah</u> (1925 reprinted in <u>The Cross in the OT</u> SCM 1955). *<u>J. Woods'</u> expository commentary (EPC 1964) is worth picking up.

An important development in the study of the book is the traditio-historical work of E.W. Nicholson in <u>Preaching to the Exiles</u> (1970 Schocken) which is suggestive for an appreciation of the kerygmatic intention of the narratives in Jeremiah - if its critical approach is right! <u>Nicholson</u> has also completed the CBC commentary on chapters 1-25 *(1973) and 26-52 *(1975).

Between 1959 and 1968 H.L. Ellison contributed a long series of articles to <u>The Evangelical Quarterly</u> which in effect comprise an exegetical commentary on Jeremiah worth of setting alongside those mentioned in the first paragraph above.

LAMENTATIONS

A full length commentary on the five poems has been contributed
by <u>D.R. Hillers</u> (Doubleday 1973), helpful for linguistic exegesis, the
structure of the poems and theology. <u>G.A.F. Knight</u> (Esther, Song of
Songs, Lamentations, Macmillan 1953) has written a useful short theological
exegesis. Not a commentary as such but a valuable study of the poetic and
theological sides of the book is N.K. Gottwald's <u>Studies in Lamentations</u>
(Allenson 1954); the theological exegesis is supplemented by the chapter
on theology in B. Albrektson's <u>Studies in the Text and Theology of
Lamentations</u> (1963 Gleerup, Lund). <u>Harrison's</u> commentary (see above under
'Jeremiah') also covers Lamentations. On <u>Gordis</u>, see under 'Song of Songs;
on <u>Fuerst</u> see under 'Ruth'; on <u>Schaeffer</u> see under 'Jeremiah'.

EZEKIEL[+]

Ezekiel has in some ways been rehabilitated now that his priestly
background and unusual behaviour are no longer held against him. Among
commentaries, pride of place must be given (at least until the translation
of <u>Zimmerli</u> in the Hermeneia series) to <u>W. Eichrodt</u> (Westminster 1970):
text, tradition history, exegesis, theology, application, are all covered.
Though you may disagree with his critical approach (there is a tendency
to write-off what is deemed expansion) this is a masterpiece. Yet <u>J.B.
Taylor</u> (IVP 1969) is by no means rendered superflous by it; often in fact
he answers the more down to earth questions we might hesitate to ask
Eichrodt (e.g. the interpretation of chapters 40-48), who is almost
Olympian; Taylor is easier to use and most lucid. And if it were not for
these two we might be more grateful for <u>D.M.G. Stalker</u> (Harper & Row
1968), in itself a quite adequate aid to the exegesis of Ezekiel and <u>J.W.
Wevers</u> (Attic Press 1969); whose detailed notes on exegetical questions are
good. A shorter introduction, working through the book paragraph by

paragraph is provided by H.L. Ellison (1956 Eerdmans) who manifests his characteristic Jewish/Christian insight.

Of older works, G.A. Cooke (Allenson 1936) remains important for textual and linguistic matters; A.B. Davidson's original CBSC volume (1892 is worth picking up; and from still earlier P. Fairbairn (1851 Baker) is still a helpful aid to following the thread of the argument, though he has been described as stodgy. Still perhaps the best popular introduction to Ezekiel is provided by H.W. Robinson in Two Hebrew Prophets (Lutterworth 1948).

DANIEL[+]

J.A. Montgomery (Allenson 1927) remains standard for textual and linguistic exegesis. E.W. Heaton (Allenson 1956) offers a thorough verse by verse exegesis, clearly expressed; the older exegetical commentaries of S.R. Driver (CUP 1900) and R.H. Charles (OUP 1913 also his bigger 'critical and exegetical commentary', 1929) are also still of value, and the treatment in Peake is good. But on a book such as this the conservativ commentaries by E.J. Young (1973 Eerdmans) and *J. Walvoord (Moody) and Leon Wood (Zondervan) should be noted for their exegesis from an evangelica viewpoint. G.H. Lang (Kregel 1973) and H. Leupold (Baker) might be mention for a conservative treatment. Themelios Vol. 2 No. 2 (1977) contains three articles on the interpretation of Daniel. R. Hammer (CBC) is due.

None of these is as warm, however, as N.W. Porteous (OTL 1965). He assumes, rather than argues for, a second-century date and concentrates on elucidating the message of the chapters, though he is at the same time demanding in his discussion of scholarly theories. More directly expositor is *A.C. Welch's Visions of the End (Attic Press 1922), which expounds both Daniel and Revelation in the light of the postwar situation. There is an article by Rowley on the message of Daniel in Interpretation 14:4 (1966)

and a substantial discussion of the book's message in the book by Bickermann
mentioned under 'Esther'.

On apocalyptic, apart from the articles in the NBD and IDB which are
both good, mention should be made of Leon Morris's Apocalyptic (1972
Eerdmans), Rowley's The Relevance of Apocalyptic (Lutterworth 1944), K.
Koch The Rediscovery of Apocalyptic (Allenson 1972) - the concern of this
book is not directly with the OT but it provides a useful orientation to
current interest of apocalyptic - and D.S. Russell's The Method and Message
of Jewish Apocalyptic (1964 Westminster); also of the essays in Journal for
Theology and Church 6 (1969) and Interpretation 25:4 (1971). See also P.
Hanson's The Relevance of Apocalyptic (1975 Fortress).

THE TWELVE PROPHETS

Although for textual and linguistic thoroughness the three ICC
volumes have not been emulated, they are more dated than average for the OCC
(W.R. Harper on Amos and Hosea 1905, J.M.P. Smith, W.H. Ward and J.A.
Bewer on Micah, Zephaniah, Nahum, Habakkuk, Obadiah, Joel, 1911; H.G.
Mitchell, J.M.P.Smith and J.A. Bewer on Haggai, Zechariah, Malachi, Jonah
1912). The EPC cover the Twelve in two little volumes, by N.H. Snaith
(Amos, Hosea, and Micah 1956) and *S.L. Edgar (1962) - the latter is
especially brief. T. Laetsch has provided a conservative commentary (1956
Concordia). IB of the Twelve includes some of the better parts of the
IB OT. G.A Smith wrote a famous expository commentory on these books
(1896-8), to which the same remarks apply as were made above with reference
to his work on Isaiah. Older and precritical, but still valued for its
devotional and homiletic insights, is E.B. Pusey's 'explanatory and
practical' commentary (c. 1860 Baker). F.A. Tatford has published a whole
series of expository studies from a millenial viewpoint (Marshall).

HOSEA +

J.L. Mays (OTL 1969) has won pride of place among commentaries on Hosea
for its valuable theological treatment of the book's message, giving prominenc
to insights to be gained from form criticism. But now we must set alongside i
H.W. Wolff's volume in the Hermeneia series (Fortress 1974). Translated from
Biblischer Kommentar it begins as a detailed commentary on text and language
but takes the task of interpretation right through (beyond Mays) to considerin
the NT fulfilment of Hosea's message. Hosea is well served by thoughtful and
thought provoking commentaries: there is an earlier theological commentary
J.M. Ward (Harper 1966) and a briefer one by G.A.F. Knight (TB 1960) - though
Knight tends to hasten rather quickly into Christianizing the text for my
personal liking. *G. Campbell Morgan's exposition (Baker 1935) directly serve
the preacher. Two more technical volumes have been written by M.J. Buss
The Prophetic Word of Hosea (De Gruyter 1969), which is concerned promarily wi
a form-critical and stylistic examination of the oracles, and W. Brueggemann's
Tradition for Crisis (John Knox 1968), which again uses insights of form
criticism and even more of tradition-criticism to portray Hosea bringing
'tradition' (law, history, etc.) to bear on 'crisis' - which is what
Brueggemann sees the Christian preacher as called to do.

H. McKeating (CBC 1971) is the only short modern exegetical work (it
also includes Amos and Micah). There are two short introductions to Hosea's
message, N.H. Snaith's Mercy and Sacrifice (RBC 1953) which, as the title
implies, gives an especially thorough treatment of the value of sacrifice and
prophetic attitudes to it, and H.W. Robinson's Two Hebrew Prophets (Lutterwort
1948) a very valuable more general introduction to the man and his message.
There are also 'Studies in the Message of Hosea' by Wolff, Eichrodt, and other
in Interpretation 15:3 (1961), and an article on Hosea's marriage by Ward in
23:4 (1969) - though Rowley gives the latter problem more systematic treatment
in an article reprinted in Men of God (1963). There is a review article on
current study of Hosea in Biblical Theology Bulletin 1: 1-2 (1971). A set of

useful studies on Hosea's message has been written by D.A. Hubbard, With Bonds of Love (Eerdmans 1968). On Ellison's treatment of Hosea as part of his survey of the northern prophets, see under 'Kings'.

JOEL +

On D.R. Jones' valuable exegetical commentary see under 'Isaiah'. S.R. Driver's CBSC commentary (1897) on Joel and Amos is worth having. G.W. Ahlstrom's Joel and the Temple Cult of Jerusaleum (Brill 1971) is primarily concerned to demonstrate that the background and origin of the prophecy is the period just after the exile; it includes some exegetical material. H.W. Wolff's commentary on Joel and Amos is promised in translation soon in the Hermeneia series (Fortress). Watts is a sympathetic understanding of the six books Joel, Obadiah, Jonah, Micah, Nahum, Habakkuk, Zephaniah (CBC 1975) in the context of Israel's faith and worship. L.C. Allen (NICOT 1976) on Joel, Obadiah, Jonah, Micah looks like a very thorough and valuable commentary from a conservative viewpoint.

AMOS +

J.L. Mays provides a first rate theological treatment, a companion volume to the one on Hosea (OTL 1969). J.A. Motyer's The Day of the Lion (IVP 1975) is an exposition but there is no lack of exegesis, though there is not much application to the social ills of our own day. In contrast, B. Thorogood (TEF 1971) applies the message systematically to modern world needs; J. Marsh (TB 1959) is also concerned with application, though his is a brief treatment. Another kind of commentary altogether is E. Hammershaimb (Blackwell 1970), an exegesis of the Hebrew text which follows it closely and especially serves the needs of the less experienced Hebraist. Honeycutt (Broadman 1963) offers us an exposition. The older exegetical/philological commentary of

R.S. Cripps (1929, 2nd edition 1955 Allenson) is out of date critically.
J.D.W. Watt's Vision and Prophecy in Amos (Eerdmans 1958) comprises four
technical but not obscure chapters on 'What kind of a prophet was Amos?',
on the book's structure, on the hymn preserved in it, and on Amos' eschatolo
R. Beeley's commentary (BoT 1970) offers a simple exegesis and devotional
thoughts. H.W. Wolff's Amos the Prophet (Fortress 1973) shows wisdom influe
on Amos.

On McKeating's useful brief exegetical commentary, see under 'Hosea';
on Ward's examination of themes in Amos, see under 'Isaiah'; on Ellison's
treatment of Amos as part of his survey of the prophets of northern Israel,
see under 'Kings'; on the commentaries of Driver and another by Wolff, see
under 'Joel'.

There is a review article on current study of Amos in Biblical Theology
Bulletin 2: 3 (1972).

OBADIAH

J.H. Eaton has written a valuable exegesis of Obadiah, Nahum, Habakkuk
and Zephaniah (TB 1961). Obadiah alone is the subject of a critical exegeti
commentary by *J.D.W. Watts (Eerdmans 1969), which includes among its concern
a positive appreciation of Obadiah's theology. On Watt's CBC volume and on
Allen, see under Joel.

JONAH +

There is a brief exegesis in his usual insightful and thought-provoking
manner by G.A.F. Knight (Ruth and Jonah TB 1950) and two systematic
theological expositions by nineteenth century writers in the reformed traditi
*P. Fairbairn (1849) and H. Martin (A. Strahan 1866) - the latter, at least,
is not as dated as one might expect. A recent equivalent in this devotional

tradition is G. Bull <u>The City and the Sign</u> (Hodder 1970) - which does, however, read old-fashionedly to me (perhaps one makes allowances for books that actually were written a century ago!) But the twentieth century man should also read J. Ellul's <u>The Judgement of Jonah</u> (Eerdmans 1971). This is a systematic exposition also in the reformed theological tradition, another of his penetrating treatments of the Bible which speaks directly to modern man in a way that older books do not. (I'm not convinced about his treatment of Jonah as a type of Christ, but this only affects part of the work.)

There is an article on 'The Kerygma of Jonah' in <u>Interpretation</u> 21: 1 (1967); and a chapter on Jonah in Bickermann's <u>Four Strange Books</u> (see under 'Esther')and in Ellison's <u>The Prophets of Israel</u> (see under 'Kings') On <u>Watts</u> and <u>Allen</u>, see under 'Joel'.

MICAH +

Micah has received less attention from commentators than the other (indisputably!) eighth century prophets. Recently, however, we have a splendid theological/exegetical/kerygmatic treatment from <u>J.L. Mays</u> (OTL 1976), as well as from the promising volume by <u>Allen</u> (NICOT under 'Joel'). J. Marsh's expository commentary on Amos and Micah (TB 1959), which is in fact stronger on Micah, is valuable. There is a series of exegetical notes on Micah by D.K. Innes in <u>Evangelical Quarterly</u> 1967-9.

NAHUM, HABAKKUK, ZEPHANIAH +

<u>Eaton</u> (under 'Obadiah') will be enough for most. <u>A.B. Davidson's</u> (CBSC 1896) is worth picking up to supplement it, or <u>Watts</u> as the most recent treatment (see under 'Joel').

On Nahum, there is a detailed exegetical commentary with a theological concern by <u>W.A. Maier</u> (Concordia 1959); and on Habakkuk a valuable exposition by D.M. Lloyd-Jones (IVP 1953), <u>From Fear to Faith</u>.

A.S. Kapulrud has written a thorough study of <u>The Message of Zephaniah</u> (Oslo U.P. 1095) which concentrates on its forms, terminology, and transmission.

HAGGAI, ZECHARIAH, MALACHI

<u>J.G. Baldwin</u> (TOTC 1972) provides a thorough exegesis with many references to other writers. <u>D.R. Jones</u> (TB 1962) is of value to supplement her, though he confesses to an idiosyncratic approach. <u>T.V. Moore</u> (2 volumes Carter and Brothers or BoT 1856) has been found valuable, though in my opinion is inclined to over-exegete, e.g. the symbolism of Zechariah - as so many older commentaries do. On Haggai-Zechariah 1-8 note, as well as <u>IB</u>, the thorough exegetical treatment in Ackroyd's <u>Exile and Restoration</u>. Also, <u>H. Leupold</u> offers us a conservative commentary on Zechariah (Baker).

OLD TESTAMENT COMMENTARY SURVEY: 1981 SUPPLEMENT

by Robert L. Hubbard, Denver Seminary, TSF Bulletin Associate Editor

The present pages present a survey of significant works which have appeared
since the publication of the original Old Testament Commentary Survey. For
ready reference, the sections of the supplement are keyed to the corresponding
ones in the original survey. I acknowledge extensive consultation with the
annual book survey of Christianity Today by Carl E. Amerding and B.S. Childs'
Old Testament Books for Pastor and Teacher (Westminster, 1977), which is an
excellent bibliographic guide.

2. GENERAL RESOURCES

a) The Text: One standard text-critical work, The Text of the Old Testament by
E. Wurthewin (Eerdmans 1980), has appeared in an updated form. Four volumes
of text-critical notes titled Preliminary and Interim Report on the Hebrew
Old Testament Text Project (1973 - 1979) are now available from the American
Bible Society and of great value to advanced students of the Hebrew Bible.

b) Literary Questions: Additions to the Fortress Press series "Guides to
Biblical Scholarship" offer introductions to areas of critical inquiry:
The Old Testament and the Historian (J.M. Miller 1976), The Old Testament and
the Literary Critic (D.A. Roberston 1977), and The Historical-Critical Method
(E. Krentz 1975). A useful survey of the development of Old Testament study
is to be found in R.E. Clements, One Hundred Years of Old Testament Interpretation (Westminster 1976). G.W. Anderson, Tradition and Interpretation (Oxford
1979) replaces Rowley's popular The Old Testament and Modern Study as a
summary of "the state of the art" in Old Testament technical research, while
J.H. Hayes, An Introduction to Old Testament Study (Abingdon 1979) surveys the
History with an eye toward informing the student of current methods in studying
the O.T.

B.S. Childs, _Introduction to the Old Testament as Scripture_ (Fortress 1979), represents a new and totally refreshing approach to "OT survey" which interprets not only the OT's literary development but the theological meaning of its present form ("canonical shape"). In my judgment, its uniqueness requires it to be used along with another standard OT introduction.

For the evangelical student wrestling with problems of modern biblical criticism, a recently published convenient source is _Biblical Criticism: Historical, Literary, and Textual_ (Zondervan 1978) by R.K. Harrison, B. Waltke, D. Guthrie, and G. Fee. Take notice also of evangelical English professor Leland Ryken's _The Literature of the Bible_ (Zondervan 1980) which offers stimulating literary studies of selected biblical sections.

c) _Language and Translation_: The _New International Version_ translation is now out and offers a refreshing new rendering of Scripture by an international team of evangelicals. Also available is one volume of a projected four-volume _NIV Interlinear Hebrew-English OT_ (ed. J. Kohlengerger III, Zondervan 1980) as is the useful _Reader's Hebrew-English Lexicon of the OT_, Vol. 1 (Genesis - Deuteronomy; ed T. Armstrong, D. Busby, C. Carr; Zondervan 1980) which lists all words in a passage occurring 50 times or less. All words and phrases are listed in the volumes on Genesis and Exodus in _The Analytical Key to the OT_ (ed. J.Owens; Harper and Row 1977, 1978). The venerable _RSV_ is now under revision.

d) _Exegesis and Background_: A massive treasure trove of literary, cultural and historical background comes in Roland de Vaux, _The Early History of Israel_ (Westminter 1978), which covers the period from Israel's beginnings to that of the judges. A similar treasury is the _Expositor's Bible Commentary_ whose Vol. 1 (ed. F. Gaebelein, Zondervan 1979) contains thirty-five articles by evangelicals on basic introductory literary, theological and historical matters. Volume one of the revised _International Standard Bible Encyclopedia_ (ed. G. Bromiley, Eerdmans 1979), an invaluable resource for Bible study, is now out with volume two expected to appear in 1981. Two well-known works are to appear soon in updated form: John Bright's A History of Israel (3rd ed., Westminster 1981) and J.A. Thompson's The Bible and Archeology (Eerdmans 1981). As an alternative to many critical theories, Israeli historian Y. Kaufmann's Religion of Israel now has a sequel which covers from the Babylonain exile to the close of the canon and argues for an early pre-exilic monotheism (The History of the Religion of Israel, KTAV 1978). A worthwhile contribution on socio-political issues is Tribes of Yahweh by N. Gottwald (Orbis, 1979). K.A. Kitchen presents a conven- ient survey of archeological finds including those of Ebla in The Bible in Its World: The Bible and Archeology Today (IVP 1978). Preliminary coverage of Ebla's materials will soon be available from the scholars involved in P. Matthiae, Ebla. An Empire Rediscovered, and G. Pettinato and M. Dahood, The Archives of Elba (both Doubleday 1981). For students without Pritchard's weighty Ancient Near Eastern Texts, an alternative translation of religious text appears in W. Beyerlin (ed.), Near Eastern Religious Texts Relating to the OT (OTL, Westmin- ster 1978). For Ugaritic literature, see M. Coogan (ed.), Stories from Ancient Canaan (Westminster 1978).

f) Theology: Vols. 3 and 4 of the Theological Dictionary of the OT, ed. Botterweck and Ringgren (Eerdmans) are now out. Soon to appear is the two-volume Theological Wordbook of the OT (ed. B. Waltke, G. Archer, and R.L. Harris; Moody 1981) which represents a substantial evangelical attempt to meet a long-recognized need.

Two major OT theologies have appeared recently which reflect standard higher critical views and at the same time offer fruitful theological insight for the serious student. It remains to be seen whether either will dislodge Eichrodt or Von Rad from their place of prominence as textbooks. In his Elusive Presence (Harper and Row 1978), S. Terrien expounds the OT and its relationship to the NT on the basis of God's elusive but pervasive presence. The center for Zimmerli's OT Theology in Outline (John Knox 1978) is the revelation of the name Yahweh. Focusing more on problems of method, R. Clement's OT Theology: A Fresh Approach (Attic 1978) opts for God himself as the unifying center of the OT. John L.

50

McKenzie's <u>A Theology of the OT</u> (Doubleday, 1974) is an impressive work by a prolific Roman Catholic scholar.

In his <u>Toward an OT Theology</u> (Zondervan 1978), evangelical Kaiser argues for the conscious development of the OT around the theme of "promise." Though not a fully developed theology, it nevertheless models a fruitful approach to this perplexing subject. For one seeking a good non-technical treatment, W. Dryness, <u>Themes in OT Theology</u> (IVP 1979) is just the book. A major OT theology by evangelical E. Martens is expected soon.

Two series of studies now offer theological reflection on specific subjects. From Fortress Press come the following "Overtures to Biblical Theology" (all paperbacks): <u>Biblical Perspectives on Death</u> (L. Bailey 1978), <u>Blessing: In the Bible and the Life of the Church</u> (C. Westermann 1978), <u>God and the Rhetoric of Sexuality</u> (P. Trible 1978), <u>Israel in Exile: A Theological Interpretation</u> (R. Klein 1979), <u>The Land: Place as Gift, Promise, and Challenge in Biblical Faith</u> (W. Brueggemann 1977), and <u>The Ten Commandments and Human Rights</u> (W. Harrelson 1980). Similarly, Abingdon offers its "Biblical Encounter Series" (all paperbcks, too): <u>Suffering</u> (E. Gerstenberger and W. Schrage 1980), <u>Festival and Joy</u> (E. Otto and T. Schramm 1980), and <u>World and Environment</u> (O. Steck 1980).

g) Exposition: The long-standing need for a basic book on exegesis is now ably met by D. Stuart, <u>Old Testament Exegesis: A Primer for Students and Pastors</u> (Westminster 1980) which incorporates practical method with an annotated bibliography. An alternative exegetical approach which aims to guide the Bible student from exegesis to sermon construction is to appear in W. Kaiser, <u>Toward An Exegetical Theology</u> (Baker 1981). Examples of insightful preaching from none less than G. von Rad himself comprise <u>Biblical Interpretations in Preaching</u> (Abingdon 1977).

Students wishing to reflect on exegetical method in the wake of Childs, <u>Biblical Theology in Crisis</u>, will be stimulated by P. Stuhlmacher, <u>Historical Criticism and Theological Interpretation of Scripture</u> (Fortress 1977) and J. Smart, <u>The Past, Present, and Future of Biblical Theology</u> (Westminster 1979).

A major contribution to the recent hermeneutical discussion this side of Gadamer comes in A. Thistleton, The Two Horizons (Eerdmans 1980).

Not to be overlooked by serious Bible students are the Fortress "Proclamation Commentaries." Influenced by the standard higher critical views of today, these volumes provide helpful literary, historical, and theological background with an eye toward preaching and teaching. Now available (all paperback): Deuteronomy, Jeremiah, (E. Achtemeier 1978), The Eighth Century Prophets: Amos, Hosea, Isaiah, Micah (B.W. Anderson 1978); Ezekiel, Second Isaiah (J.L. Mays 1978); Genesis, Exodus, Leviticus, Numbers (F. McCurley 1979); Joshua, Judges, Samuel, Kings (W. Rast 1978), The Psalms, Job (R. Murphy 1977).

3. ONE VOLUME COMMENTARIES AND SERIES

The caliber of contributors to The New Layman's Bible Commentary in One Volume (ed. G. Howley, F.F. Bruce, H.L. Ellison; Zondervan 1979) make it an up-to-date, useful exposition of the Bible. Note that the NCB is being published in paperback by Eerdmans. See also the "Proclamation Commentaries" listed above.

4. COMMENTARIES BOOK BY BOOK - THE PENTATEUCH

Two important works on the Pentateuch merit mention. D.J.A. Clines, The Theme of Pentateuch (Univ. of Sheffield 1979), provides a short but stimulating exposition of the Pentateuch as a whole. H.L. Ellison's Fathers of the Covenant: Genesis and Exodus (Paternoster 1979) brings together twelve articles published earlier which skillfully blend scholarship and devotion into good reading. "The Torah: A Modern Commentary Series" (UAHC) represents excellent Jewish scholarship.

Those struggling to take Genesis literally yet avoid the excessive "young earth" of the militant creationists will benefit from R. Newman and H. Eckelmann, Genesis One and the Origin of the Earth (IVP 1977). Both scholar and layman will profit from Catholic scholar B. Vawter's On Genesis (Doubleday 1977), a weighty discussion of that book's theology, compositional origin, and relevance for today followed by line-by-line comment. C. Westermann's The Promises to the Fathers (Fortress 1980) constitutes an erudite exposition of that motif--a must for the serious student but very heavy reading for others. Though very dated, the recently reprinted two volumes by F. Delitzsch (Klock and Klock 1978) are still valuable for theological reflection.

EXODUS

G.A.F. Knight interprets this book under the theme of revelation in his Theology as Narration (Eerdmans 1977). Valuable for its relevance to the current criticism of a thirteenth century exodus date, J. Bimson's Redating the Exodus and Conquest (University of Sheffield 1978) argues ably for the traditional fifteenth century date. J.P. Hyatt's NCB volume is now available in paperback (Eerdmans 1980). Moshe Greenberg's Understanding Exodus (Behrman 1969, o.p.) represents excellent Jewish scholarship, and will soon be updated (UAHC).

LEVITICUS

Two evangelical commentaries of this often overlooked book are now out. R.K. Harrison (IVP 1980) maintains the high standard of scholarship and spiritual insight of the TOTC series. A more ambitious work is the newest NICOT volume, G.Wenham (Eerdmans 1979), which offers a fresh, thorough interpretation of the book and its applicability for Christians daily living without getting hopelessly bogged down in critical questions. Another Jewish work, this one by Bamberger, is very good (UAHC 1979).

DEUTERONOMY

A.D.H. Mayes' contribution to the rather stodgy NCB series will appear soon in paperback (Eerdmans 1981).

5. THE 'HISTORIES'

JOSHUA

The NICOT volume by M. Woudstra was just released (Eerdmans 1981) and will, no doubt, continue that series' tradition of evangelical scholarship at its best.

Ministers will find the reprint of W.G. Blaikie (Klock and Klock 1978) useful for sermon preparation.

JUDGES

J.A. Soggin's contribution to the OTL is soon to be published (Westminster 1981). It remains to be seen whether the preoccupation with literary questions over theological reflection so characteristic of his Joshua volume will be true here, too. The form and lessons of the Samson story are interpreted provocatively by J.L. Crenshaw in Samson: A Secret Betrayed, A Vow Ignored (John Knox 1978). A substantial presentation of the lives of various judges in a devotional format comes in Gary Inrig, Hearts of Iron--Feet of Clay (Moody 1979).

RUTH

J.M. Sasson's (John Hopkins 1979) is heavy on translation and often questionable philology, weak on theological interest.

SAMUEL

The AB volume on this book by P.K. McCarter, Jr. (Doubleday 1980) follows the series' original format, i.e., a new translation with philological notes and comment but little theological reflection. The recently reprinted volumes by W.G. Blaikie, on I and II Samuel (Klock and Klock 1978) are valuable for those interested in preaching. Several scholarly monographs treat specific subjects: B. Birch, The Rise of the Israelite Monarchy (Scholars Press 1976) traces the growth and development of the I Samuel 7-15, while J.R. Vannoy in Covenant Renewal at Gilgal (Mack Publishing Co. 1978) claims to have found a covenant form in I Sam. 11:14-12:25 which resolves the alleged pro- and antimonarchial tensions there. D.M. Gunn analyzes the structure of the "succession narrative" in The Story of King David (University of Sheffield 1979).

KINGS

A valuable but simplified edition of E.R. Thiele's classic work on OT chronology is now available in paperback as A Chronology of the Hebrew Kings (Zondervan 1977). The reprint of F.W. Farrar's commentaries on the Kings (Klock and Klock 1980) offers solid exegesis from the Victorian era.

CHRONICLES, EZRA, NEHEMIAH

Respected evangelical scholar D. Kidner has contributed to the TOTC (Ezra and Nehemiah, IVP 1979). R.J. Coggins ably interprets all three books theologically in his addition to the CBC (CUP 1976).

ESTHER

Sandra Berg (Scholars Press 1979) offers a fresh, illuminating study of this neglected book's structure, motifs, and themes.

6. THE POETICAL BOOKS

From the pen of evangelical C.H. Bullock comes An Introduction to the OT Poetical Books (Moody 1979), a thoroughly conservative treatment of the critical problems and major themes of this canonical section. For the serious student, two collections of essays treat more technical aspects of recent wisdom literature research: J.L. Crenshaw ed., Studies in Ancient Israelite Wisdom (KTAV 1976), and J.G. Gammie ed. Israelite Wisdom: Theological and Literary Essays in Honor of Samuel Terrien (Scholars Press 1978). L.G. Perdue's Wisdom and Cult (Scholars Press 1977) offers a technical but very readable analysis of the attitude toward cult in both biblical and ancient Near Eastern wisdom. Finally, soon to appear is R. Murphy's Wisdom Literature (Eerdmans 1981), the first of a multi-volume form-cirtical encyclopedia called "Forms of the OT." This volume handles Ruth, Esther, Job, Proverbs, Ecclesiastes, and Canticles, and, if its author is any indicator, will be a "must" for the serious student's library.

JOB

A massive treasury of learning and theological insight (600 pages!) -- the flower of one scholar's life-long endeavors -- is R. Gordis (KTAV 1978). No good student will want to miss this one. The reprint of E.C. Sumner (Klock and Klock 1978) is exegetically and homiletically useful for the pastor. Also useful for their homiletical and devotional content are W.B. Ewing's Job

A Vision of God (Seabury 1976) and John Calvin's Sermons from
Job (Baker 1979), a translation of some of that great reformer's expositions.
An NCB volume in paperback by H.H. Rowley will soon appear (Eerdmans 1981).
Form criticism and theological insight at their best are expected in C. Westermann's
brief The Structure of Job: A Form Critical Analysis (Fortress 1981).

PSALMS

The reprint of sixteenth century Puritan D. Dickson's commentary (2 vols.,
Klock and Klock 1978) is highly recommended for its solid exegesis and warm
devotional content. A popular presentation of form-critical psalm types appears
in J.H. Hayes, Understanding the Psalms (Judson 1976). D.A. Hubbard's More
Psalms for All Seasons (Eerdmans 1976) offers useful interpretation of selected
psalms in sermonic form. J. Goldingay's Songs from a Strange Land, newest of
the "The Bible Speaks Today" series, combines solid exegesis and insightful
contemporary application of Psalms 42-51. A. MacLaren's three-volumes are to be
offered soon as a reprint (Klock and Klock 1981) and represents Victorian
preaching at its best. A good Roman Catholic commentary by L. Sabourin, The
Psalms: Their Origin and Meaning, is also available (Alba House 1969, 2 vols.).

SONG OF SONGS

M. Pope's contribution to the AB departs from the series' original format and
provides a massive, detailed commentary which roots this book in the sacred
marriage rites of the ancient Near Eastern fertility cult (Doubleday 1977).
With a cautious eye towards its eccentricities the student will find it provoc-
ative reading. J.B. White, on the other hand, argues in A Study of the Language
of Love in the Song of Songs and Ancient Egyptian Poetry (Scholars Press 1978)
that the book consists of lyrical love songs much like Egyptian poetry.

7. THE PROPHETS

Interest in prophetic literature continues unabated. Useful summary articles
on the subject appeared in Interpretation 32, No. 1 (1978). Of a more technical

nature are articles treating the sociology of prophecy and the canonical development of prophetic books in G. Coats and B. Long (eds.), Canon and Authority (Fortress 1977). R.R. Wilson offers a major, technical study of prophecy in his Prophecy and Society in Ancient Israel (Fortress 1980). A very excellent reply to the Hal Lindsey approach has been authored by Dewey Beegle, Prophecy and Prediction (Pryor Pettengil 1978). A more popular response is J. Limburg, The Prophets and The Powerless (John Knox 1977).

A very readable survey of the origin, nature, message, and methods of prophecy is H. Mowvley, Reading the OT Prophets Today (John Knox 1979). A more conservative book-by-book treatment of the prophets is Leon Wood's posthumously published The Prophets of Israel (Baker 1979).

JEREMIAH

The long-lamented absence of a solid commentary on this book is now ably met by J.A. Thompson (NICOT: Eerdmans 1980). Thoroughly informed, insightful, and evangelical, this volume is a "must." Similarly informed yet homiletically oriented, A.W. Blackwwod (Word 1977) will be of immense help to the pastor. The serious student will find in W.L. Holladay's The Architecture of Jeremiah 1-20 (Bucknell Univ. 1976) a stimulating analysis of the growth of that material. Not to be overlooked for theological insight is J. Bright's Covenant and Promise (Westminster 1976).

EZEKIEL

The publication in translation of W. Zimmerli's massive work in the Hermeneia series (Fortress 1979) is cause for celebration. Though one may disagree with some of its critical positions, this volume's awesome erudition and theological insight make it the best commentary available on Ezekiel 1-24. P. Fairbairn's reprinted Exposition of Ezekiel (Klock and Klock 1978) is useful for its devotional content and review of earlier interpretations of this book. J.D. Levenson's dissertation, Theology of the Program of Restoration of Ezekiel 40-48 (Scholars Press 1977), provides the more scholarly-minded with a stimulating exposition of those unusual chapters.

DANIEL

J. Baldwin's TOTC contribution (IVP 1978), is another "must" purchase. Erudite yet relevant to today, it will help students and pastors understand this enigmatic book. So also will R. Wallace's The Lord is King: The Message of Daniel (IVP 1979), a well-informed exposition in the "The Bible Speaks Today" series. Another thorough, relevant, conservative commentary is offered by Desmond Ford (Southern Publishing Assoc., Nashville 1979). Though attributing less historical validity to Daniel than the above volumes, two other major commentaries present much useful material: A. Lacocque (John Knox 1978) and L.E. Hartman and A. KiLella (AB: Doubleday 1978). For the serious student, mention should be made of J.J. Collins' dissertation, The Apocalyptic Vision of the Book of Daniel (Scholars Press 1978).

HOSEA

The AB volume by F.I. Andersen and D.N. Freedman (Doubleday 1980), looks excellent--thorough in erudition, somewhat theological in orientation. Though this Anchor Series does not bill itself as "commentaries," this volume offers more than most.

JOEL

The long-awaited Hermeneia volume by H.W. Wolff, on is now out (Fortress 1977). Respresenting form criticism at its best, it will become a standard work alongside Mays' well-known volume on Amos.

AMOS

T. Fretheim's The Message of Jonah (Augsburg 1977) is a thorough, delightfully written exposition of this book which combines excellent literary analysis with rich theological insight. Less thorough yet insightful is H.W. Wolff, Jonah: Church in Revolt (Clayton Publishing House 1979).

MICAH

If an author's reputation is any indicator, H.W. Wolff's soon-to-be-published book on Micah should be of great value (Fortress 1981).

NAHUM, HABAKKUK, ZEPHANIAH

A well-written theological interpretation of Habakkuk as a theodicy is D.E. Gowan's *The Triumph of Faith in Habakkuk* (John Knox 1976). A. and P. LePeau and J. Stewart offer a popular presentation of the book for students in *Just Living By Faith* (IVP 1979).

SOME 'BEST BUYS' (1981 Update)

<u>One volume commentaries and series</u>   NBC Revised, or <u>The New Laymans Bible</u>
   <u>Commentary</u>.

<u>GENESIS</u>   Initially perhaps Kidner and Sarna; but von Rad, Thielicke, Speiser,
   Richardson, Westermann and some of the others are also ones you may not
   be able to resist buying when you have sampled them.

<u>EXODUS</u>   Begin with Cole and Childs, then G. Henton Davies and Driver (which is
   actually at least as substancial as McNeile though it does not appear so).

<u>LEVITICUS, NUMBERS</u>   Wenham (NICOT) or Harrison (TOTC).

<u>DEUTERONOMY</u>   Thompson, Cunliffe-Jones and Clement's <u>God's Chosen People</u>.

<u>JOSHUA</u>   Woudstra (see Calvin; article in JBL 90.2, 1971).

<u>JUDGES</u>   Cundall and Hercus.

<u>RUTH</u>   Knight, Fuerst, Morris.

<u>SAMUEL</u>   Hertzberg, also Hercus and McKane.

<u>KINGS</u>   see von Rad <u>Theology I</u> and Ellul <u>Politics of God</u>.

<u>CHRONICLES, EZRA, NEHEMIAH</u>   Ackroyd, Kidner (TOTC), Coggins

<u>ESTHER</u>   Knight, Fuerst.

<u>THE POETICAL BOOKS</u>   von Rad <u>Wisdom in Israel</u>, Murphey's <u>Wisdom Literature</u>

<u>JOB</u>   Andersen; also for overview Jones or Wood or H.W. Robinson or Ellison
   or T.H. Robinson.

<u>PSALMS</u>   Weiser (OTL) and Kidner (TOTC) or Eaton (TB) and Andersen (NCB).

<u>PROVERBS</u>   Kidner (TOTC); then ask a rich uncle to buy you McKane (OTL)!

<u>ECCLESIASTES</u>   Gordis, Kidner.

<u>SONG OF SONGS</u>   Knight, Fuerst, Gordis.

<u>THE PROPHETS</u>   von Rad, Hercus, Mowvly

<u>ISAIAH</u>   Mauchline and Westermann; then Kaiser (especially on 1-12); North's
   <u>Second Isaiah</u>, and Jones - or one of the expositions.

<u>JEREMIAH</u>   Harrison (TOTC), Thompson (NICOT).

<u>LAMENTATIONS</u>   Gottwald, Knight, Fuerst, Gordis.

<u>APOCOLYPTIC LITERATURE</u>   Morris.

EZEKIEL   Taylor and Eichrodt, or save up for Zimmerli.

DANIEL   Baldwin (TOTC), then Porteous and Young.

HOSEA   Andersen and Freedman (AB) then Mays, Knight, Wolff, Morgan.

JOEL   Allen, Jones, Watts, or save for Wolff.

AMOS   Mays, Thorogood, or Wolff.

OBADIAH   Allen, Eaton, Watts (CBC).

JONAH   Knight, Ellul, Watts, Allen.

MICAH   Mays, Allen.

NAHUM, HABAKKUK, ZEPHANIAH   Eaton, Watts, Lloyd-Jones.

HAGGAI, ZECHARIAH, MALACHI   Baldwin.